Bella Webb is a barrister at Old Square Chambers. She has 18 years of experience with a flourishing practise in the clinical negligence and clinical regulatory fields, as well as undertaking broader personal injury work. She is used to working on high value and sensitive claims, where her empathetic, compassionate and professional approach allows her clients (be they Claimant or Defendant) to feel as at ease as possible and to have total confidence in her expertise. Delayed cancer claims are a particular specialism and an area in which Bella has been developing her practise with great success in recent years. It is a subject upon which she speaks regularly.

Bella is credited in the Legal 500 as an advocate who "*inspires confidence in clients.*" (2015) and someone who "*...is incredibly approachable and clients appreciate her warm and understanding approach.*" (2017).

A Practical Guide to Claims Arising from Delays in Diagnosing Cancer

A Practical Guide to Claims Arising from Delays in Diagnosing Cancer

Bella Webb
MA (Hons) Jurisprudence (Oxon),
Barrister at Law, Old Square Chambers (London),
Clinical Negligence, Clinical Regulatory, Personal Injury

Law Brief Publishing

Published 2018 by Law Brief Publishing, an imprint of Law Brief Publishing Ltd
30 The Parks
Minehead
Somerset
TA24 8BT

www.lawbriefpublishing.com

Paperback: 978-1-911035-98-5

For Freya

PREFACE

Cancer is sadly one of the most prevalent diseases (or group of diseases) in modern society, and remains the most common cause of death for men and women in England and Wales, according to ONS statistics. It is also a byword for fear and will probably have touched almost every person reading this text in one way or another. With the technological advances of the internet and social media, and the increased propensity (quite properly) for patients to take control of their health and treatment, rather than deferring unquestioningly to the medical profession, it is perhaps not surprising that legal claims arising out of the misdiagnosis or delayed diagnosis of cancer subtypes appear to be on the rise. And yet, there has been surprisingly little written about what is, albeit a niche topic, such a broad and important area of practise in the clinical law sphere. I was therefore delighted to be tasked with producing this book to assist legal practitioners in the practical management of these complex, emotive and fascinating cases. I sincerely hope that this book will be of interest and assistance to all of those undertaking work in this field, whether for claimant or defendant and regardless of their level of expertise.

The law as discussed within the book is accurate as at 1st October 2018. There are of course ongoing advances in medicine, and a considerable investment in the development of new cancer tests, diagnostic tools, and treatment options. It is hoped that these initiatives will change the cancer tide in the nearer rather than the more distant future, and with it, the legal role within cancer claims.

I would like to thank my parents and my husband and beautiful daughter, who have been a constant support to me through the process of writing this book and in everything that I do. I could not have got where I am now without them. I would also like to thank my clerks and colleagues in chambers for providing a ready ear and advice when needed.

Bella Webb
October 2018

PREFACE

CONTENTS

Chapter One	Introduction	1
Chapter Two	The History and the Science	5
	The History	5
	League Tables and Audits	6
	The Science	8
	Grade and Stage	12
	i. Grade	
	ii. Stage and Staging Systems	
	Doubling Times	13
	Summary	15
Chapter Three	The Opening Review of a Case – Use of Guidelines and Statistics	19
	First Steps	20
	Reviewing the Medical Records	20
	Witness Evidence	21
	The NICE Guidelines	22
	How to Maximise Breach of Duty Submissions	30
	Summary	37
Chapter Four	Different Types of Cancer and Their Varied Legal Impact	41
	Multiple Consultations	41
	Why are Some Cancers More Likely to Require Multiple Consultations?	43
	How Does This Affect Breach of Duty?	45
	Summary	47
Chapter Five	Experts	49
	Expert Selection	49
	The Right Experts?	50
	Instructing the Experts	53
	Summary	57

Chapter Six	Causation	59
	Factual Causation	59
	The Pitfalls of Expert Causation Evidence	61
	Reliance upon Data for Differing Cancer Types or Reliance Upon Data at the Expense of Histology and Symptom Presentation	62
	Life Expectancy Data	66
	Summary	70
Chapter Seven	Legal Causation	73
	Causation in a Clinical Negligence Setting	73
	Loss of Chance	74
	Lost Years Claims	77
	Material Contribution? The Future?	82
	Summary	86
Chapter Eight	Client Care and Framing the Case	89
	Sensitivity	89
	Framing the Case – How and When to bring Proceedings	91
	The Primary Options	93
	Provisional Damages	94
	Periodical Payments	98
	Taxation	100
	Drafting Complexities	101
	Summary	102

CHAPTER ONE
INTRODUCTION

Cancer is a hot topic and is likely to remain as such for the foreseeable future. It is a sad fact that, according to Office of National Statistics ("ONS") data regarding deaths registered in 2016 (and released in July 2017), cancer remained the most common cause of death for both women and men when assessed on a broad disease group level. Generically, cancer accounted for 28.5% of all deaths registered in 2016. Within the cancer subset, ONS statistics indicate that lung cancer remains the biggest killer.

It is perhaps self-evident that, as a result of the fact that cancer is such a significant cause of death, the economic cost of cancer diagnoses is massive. Zurich's claims statistics for the period from January to June 2017 inclusive taken from the website www.futureproofinsurance.co.uk, indicate that Zurich paid out some £121.6 million to around 2000 customers during that period. Of those pay-outs, cancer was by far the most common reason for payment being made, accounting for approximately 53% of claims. Breast cancer alone accounted for approximately 30% of claims made. Similarly, on Aegon's website, an analysis of claims data on 26th March 2018, revealed that cancer made up 42% of deaths leading to successful life protection claims comprising 97% of terminal illness claims, 60% of critical illness claims and 29% of income protection claims. Of the terminal illness claims, lung related cancers were the single most common subtype, accounting for 28% of pay-outs, followed in second place by bowel and rectal cancers.

We live in increasingly litigious times. No doubt in part due to the significant role of the media in our daily lives, and the rapid growth of technology and social media, the average person is far more aware of their rights and the avenues open to them for redress, should there be a suspicion of "blame" in respect of negative life events. It is both easy and likely more common for the average person to enter details of their symptoms and ultimate diagnoses into an internet search engine and discover aspects of their disease, as well as any publicised criticism of care surrounding such diagnoses that, just a couple of decades ago, were not readily accessible to members of the public. As such, many people are rather less ready to accept the word of medical professionals without question. Gone are the days when medics were given the status of deities by their patients. Interestingly, an article on www.ftadviser.com on 7th November 2016, noted that cancer claims were on the rise amongst men in particular, accounting for 50% of all male critical illness claims as reported by Aegon in 2015; an increase from 2014. Stephen Crosbie, protection director at Aegon UK, is credited as having suggested that the rise could, at least in part, be due to campaigns (in the media and elsewhere) aimed at increasing the awareness of male health issues and the importance of regular health checks. In a survey conducted by YouGov on behalf of the MPS between 9th and 10 February 2017 and reported in the MPS' "Clinical Negligence Costs – Striking a Balance" Policy paper in June 2017, 65% of those surveyed felt that it was now simpler to make a clinical negligence claim than ever before.

Perhaps therefore, we ought not to be surprised that the combination of increasing social and health awareness, together with the mortality implications of a cancer diagnosis has had a knock-on effect upon the pursuit of legal claims arising from the diagnosis (or alleged misdiagnosis) of cancer.

On 9th November 2014, the Telegraph reported that the NHS had paid out nearly £45 million to around 700 cancer patients in respect of claims brought by patients for alleged missed diagnoses brought against hospitals. The article takes those figures to show that approximately seven patients every month were wrongly being given the all clear by hospital staff. Of course, those statistics, notwithstanding the years that have since passed, do not account for the likely significant number of unrecorded cases, and the perhaps more substantial number of cases brought against general practitioners for the alleged failure to refer sufficiently early for suspected cancer symptoms. The MDU's website suggests that between January 2010 and March 2015, around 250 files per year were being opened in respect of claims relating to missed cancer diagnoses, and that although the numbers settled or successfully brought were considerably smaller, around 15% of cases in which compensation was paid between 2005 and 2014 related to delayed or missed cancer diagnosis claims. Similarly, the MPS website reports (on 23rd May 2016) that a review of their top one hundred high value claims opened during 2015 had shown that the commonest type of delayed diagnosis case related to cancer, comprising 16% of cases.

However, it is not just the economic cost of these claims that makes them so important in today's society. Cancer is also perhaps the disease (or group of diseases) which carries with it the greatest fear factor amongst the population. That is at least in part because it can be an extremely painful and degrading disease, limiting one's life expectancy and with a massive impact upon the quality of the patient's remaining life. It is not uncommon to hear survivors of the disease commenting that the treatment is at times worse than the disease itself.

Lawyers must also be well aware that all litigation is stressful and time consuming for the lay parties. In a cancer claim, where the client is either a cancer survivor, is currently suffering from the disease and undergoing treatment, a bereaved family member or on the other side of the coin, a doctor whose practise is being criticised in the most unpleasant of ways, the logistics of managing the claim and the additional stress that entails cannot be underestimated. As such, these claims, whether for claimant or defendant are about much, much more than an understanding of ***Bolam v Friern Hospital Management Committee (1957) 2 All ER 118***, or the strict letter of the law.

This book will therefore aim to equip you with the tools to deconstruct and manage these legally and often factually complex and emotive claims through to trial, and provide a practical guide to the issues that the legal practitioner will need to consider. It will guide you through the background to the history of such claims and the data which underlies them and then take you step by step through the distinctions between different cancers and the impact of cancer "type" upon how the case is run, as well as understanding the NICE guidelines and other useful sources of information. That background is invaluable to understanding why these claims are so significant and the premise upon which they are based. From those foundations, we will explore how to review a potential claim, prioritising and managing evidence through to instructing experts, considering the often crucial issues of factual and legal causation and framing claims for the seriously ill, dying and bereaved with practical approaches to the problems that such claims throw up.

It is hoped that this text will be of benefit to all clinical negligence practitioners dealing with delayed cancer diagnosis claims, whether they act for the claimant or defendant.

CHAPTER TWO
THE HISTORY AND THE SCIENCE

This chapter will look at the trend towards an increase in delayed cancer diagnosis claims and the rationale and statistics that underlie it. It will then go on to look at what we actually mean by cancer in medical terms. How does the disease operate and how is it diagnosed? A background understanding of both of these issues is essential to the management of any legal claim based upon an allegation of delayed diagnosis. If we as lawyers do not understand what cancer is and how it develops within the human body, we cannot hope to build and run an efficient and effective legal case. The application of the legal principles underlying breach of duty, causation and injury are always fact specific. This chapter will help us start to get to grips with some of the facts which permeate all cases of this type.

The History

Delayed cancer diagnosis claims are undoubtedly on the rise. Why? Cancer survival rates in the UK are a hot topic. The media have, in recent years, published articles which suggest that cancer survival in the UK is the worst anywhere in Europe. Moreover, Cancer Research UK published a report in September 2014 indicating that early diagnosis saves lives, and that late diagnosis of cancers in the UK can explain the poor survival rates in Britain compared with other countries. The same report also suggested that there was extremely wide variation in regional and local practice, accounting for nearly a threefold difference between the best and worst clinical commissioning groups.

On 30th January 2018, the CONCORD-3 report was published by the Lancet. CONCORD is the global programme for surveillance of cancer survival, led by the London School of Hygiene & Tropical Medicine. The steering committee is comprised of scientists and cancer patients from 13 countries, according to the Cancer Survival Group and

LSHTM website. It updates the statistics for survival to 2014 and includes 18 cancers and groups of cancer that collectively represent 75% of the global cancer burden.

A review of the results shows (as confirmed by LSHTM) that whilst overall cancer survival has improved and continues to do so, with some cancers such as breast cancer (increased from 80 – 86%) and rectal cancer (from 55 to 63%) showing significant increases in five year survival; the UK still lags behind other comparable countries in respect of the survival statistics for several common cancers.

There is also worrying evidence reported by the BBC and other media outlets that:

(a) Delays in diagnosis are vastly different between the richest and the poorest. That reflects not only issues with access to care but also the propensity of the patient themselves to recognise symptoms of concern and attend their GP. It is said that income, age, gender and cancer type all play a part, and;

(b) Delays are more prevalent in certain regions – perhaps reflecting the socio-economic issues considered above.

League Tables and Audits

Such has been the concern about the UK's approach to cancer diagnosis, that league tables for GPs were introduced during 2013, the first set of which appeared to find, according to articles in the media, including the Telegraph on 6th December 2013, that more than half are not referring such patients to specialists quickly enough. The national performance data – which covers all 8,000 GP practices in England – enables patients to look up their own surgery, and see how it performs against dozens of indicators about diagnosis and treatment of most of the common diseases and conditions.

It should however be noted that there is controversy about the interpretation that can properly be placed upon the results. Sean Duffy, national clinical director for cancer at NHS England, said, as reported on GP online on 9th December 2013, that the data was complex and not easy to interpret. For example, he noted that a large proportion of patients do not present to their GP with symptoms, such that cancers are only detected when the patient attends at A&E. He claimed that the statistics tell us more about how the system works as a whole. Similarly, GPC chairman Dr Chaand Nagpaul said that the tables were overly simplistic and did not show the complexity of diagnosing patients.

As recently as September 2016, a voluntary audit for GP practices was launched by a collaboration between the RCGP, Public Health England (PHE), Cancer Research UK and Macmillan. It collects data on how many cancers have been diagnosed, the types of cancers diagnosed, the number of tests and consultations GPs use and how many cancers are diagnosed late or early. The review looked first at data from 2014 and then aims to compare that to data from 2015 onwards to build a picture of how diagnosis has changed following the introduction of NICE' latest guidance on diagnosing cancer, and then compared against the national average. The first set of results at the end of 2017 appeared to show rather better figures than those suggested elsewhere. Further, in 2016, NHS England made more than £200m available to Cancer Alliances from 2016-2018 in order to develop new models of care that will speed up diagnosis.

There have been other advances. New screening tests for bowel and cervical cancer are to be introduced during 2018 and 2019 (see NHS England's website) and research continues into a universal blood test for cancer, known as the CancerSEEK test. According to an article by Alexander Castellino on 18th January 2018, published on www.medscape.com, the test will aim to look for mutations in sixteen genes that regularly arise in cancer, as well as certain proteins that are commonly released. Further, a new cancer diagnosis standard, intended to ensure that patients learn within 28 days whether or not they have cancer, will be introduced in 2020. In preparation, a new Cancer Waiting Times System will be commenced in April 2018 so that teams of clinicians can ascertain how to collect data for the new standard. NHS England reports that five sites are already piloting the new 28-day standard across six cancer pathways – gynaecology, urology, head and neck, lung, lower and upper gastrointestinal.

As noted in the introduction, no doubt one of the primary reasons for the increase in litigation surrounding delayed cancer diagnosis is the fact that the patient body are now much more knowledgeable, media savvy and willing to question the views of medics than ever before. We are regularly exposed to news stories about poor diagnosis statistics, and about symptom awareness and self-care. That can only be a good thing in real terms but simultaneously gives rise to an increasing trend towards litigation and claim awareness.

The Science

It ought to go without saying, but the basis of any successful claim or defence in the field of clinical negligence, is an understanding of the medical building blocks of the injury or disease with which one is dealing. That is especially so of cancer. It is not enough simply to rely upon one's expert or experts to tell us everything. Of course, they are vital (for which see later chapters) in establishing breach of duty and causation, and in assisting the legal team with the more intricate medical details. However, in order to get the best from one's experts, and in order to test their credibility effectively, the lawyer must themselves have a background understanding of the condition in question.

There is a tendency to view "cancer" as a single disease. That is not the case, and different types of cancer have different rules, both medically and legally speaking. Plainly, this book is not the correct place to undertake a detailed exploration of what cancer is, and nor is the author appropriately qualified to do so. However, a brief summary of the medical building blocks is required. For further reading upon the topic, there are numerous medical texts and cancer websites available to assist the lawyer in this field.

It is important to remember that cancer is in fact a collection of multiple different but associated diseases. According to the National Cancer Institute (cancer.gov website) and the Cancer Research website (cancerresearchuk.org), in all forms of the disease, a group of cells in the human body begin to divide uncontrollably and can spread into surrounding tissues. Cancer can start almost anywhere in the body. There are currently thought to be over 200 different types of cancer.

The NCI website and cancerresearchuk.org go on to tell us the following key facts:

(a) Cancer is a disease caused by changes to our genes, whether inherited or arising during our lifetime and for example, through environmental exposure to substances.

(b) Each individual's cancer has a unique pattern of genetic change. As such, it is said that even within the same type of tumour there will be differences in cells with variable genetic alterations.

(c) In normal circumstances, cells grow and divide to form new cells as and only when the body requires them.

(d) When cancer develops that order breaks down and the development of extra abnormal uncontrolled cells can form growths called tumours.

(e) A tumour may contain millions of cancer cells.

(f) Most cancers form solid tumours but others, such as blood borne cancers do not.

(g) All of the tissues of the body have a membrane to keep that tissue's unique cells inside its walls. Cancer has the ability to break through that membrane and invade other local tissues. The process by which it does so is not fully understood but it is thought that growth outwards occurs through one or more of the following:

- Pressure from the growing tumour until it forces its way through the weakest party of the normal tissue and causing the normal tissue to die off when deprived of blood and oxygen;

- The use of enzymes to break down cells;

- Direct movement of cells. Cancer cells can generally move more easily than normal cells.

(h) Tumours that are cancerous can invade surrounding structures or some cells can break off and travel to (and start growing in) remote areas through the blood or lymph systems to form secondary tumours. These secondary tumours are called metastases and they will have the same type of cancer cells as the original cancer. So for example, if a patient/claimant starts off with bowel cancer which then spreads to the lung, the secondary cancer is a metastatic bowel cancer and not lung cancer, even though it is present within the lung cells and/or tissues. The process by which the cancer spreads to distant parts of the body is called metastasis.

(i) Benign tumours do not spread in the same way and do not usually have the same propensity to return (save perhaps for some brain tumours).

(j) Cancers are most often named for the tissues or the organs which are the focus of the disease's formation. Cancer may also be described by the type of cell in which it is formed – ie: carcinoma, sarcoma, leukaemia, lymphoma etc:

A word about cancer spread. There is reference above to metastatic disease. One important point to keep in mind with cancer claims is that, as with a primary tumour, which takes time to grow and to form a tumour, so too do metastatic deposits. The name for areas of cancer spread that are, as yet, too small to be identified on a scan are micro metastases. For most cancers, Cancer Research UK remind us that there is, as yet in any event, no blood test to tell whether or not a cancer has spread, and as a result, the diagnosis of cancer spread (or its likelihood for our purposes as lawyers) is based upon a range of clinical factors, including:

(a) Experience from previous cases;

(b) If surgery has taken place to remove the primary tumour, an assessment of whether there are cancer cells in the blood vessels of the tumour;

(c) The grade of the cancer (the higher the more likely the spread), and;

(d) Analysis of the lymph nodes if removed surgically.

Whether or not there has been metastatic spread of the disease is critical in assessing treatment options and ultimately in determining survival prospects.

Some of the most obvious difficulties for the legal assessment of a delayed cancer claim will no doubt already be apparent from the quick summary of the scientific background above. In particular:

- The sheer fact that each cancer and its development and growth is unique, working on an individual genetic pattern influenced by the patient's own physiology, in combination with often multiple environmental factors, makes predictions about its rate of growth, and therefore its "likely" course but for any delay, incredibly difficult, and frequently open to controversy, and;

- The potential for there to be micro metastases, not detectable by any form of scan, allows, in some cases dealing with higher grade or larger primary tumours, the potential for speculative argument about whether the disease would in fact have spread already at any earlier proposed diagnosis date, and therefore led to the same (poorer) outcome.

Those considerations, amongst others, will be highly relevant in the assessment of expert evidence on either side and in respect of causation, which will be considered in greater detail later in this book.

Grade and Stage

Grade

The grade and stage of the cancer are largely determinative of the treatment pathway recommended, as well as the survival prospects.

In terms of grading, the grade of the cancer will be relevant to an assessment of the likelihood that it has metastasised or might metastasise and as such, an understanding of both grade and stage are key to an effective assessment of causation in any delayed cancer diagnosis claim.

The grade of a tumour indicates how abnormal its cells and tissues are when compared with the norm. Whilst there are different types of grading systems, generally speaking there are three grades, with grade 1 indicative of a cancer which looks similar to normal cells and grows slowly, and grade three being the most abnormal and rapidly developing. The grade of a cancer does not change over time.

Stage and Staging Systems

The stage of a cancer is slightly different. Staging describes both size of tumour and the extent of its growth. Again, there are different types of staging system in place for different cancers – for example melanomas may be measured for their Breslow thickness, colorectal cancers have a Dukes stage and for prostate cancer the stage is a measure of the extent of growth or invasion and the Gleason grade is a measure of the aggressiveness of the cancer.

However, probably the most detailed and common staging system is the Tumour, Node, Metastasis (TNM) system, which was developed by the American Joint Committee on Cancer (AJCC) and the Union for International Cancer Control (UICC). Their website, https://cancerstaging.org explains the system in detail. The size of the tumour is usually measured in centimetres and it is the size of the primary tumour which generally determines its T stage. T1 represents the smallest size and T2, T3 and T4 represent progressively larger tumours depending upon their spread to nearby tissues.

As described previously, at some stage in cancer development, some cancer cells may migrate from the primary tumour and spread to the lymph nodes. The nodes may swell and the size of the lymph nodes and / or extent of the spread is categorised by "N" in the TNM scale. N0 represents no lymph node spread with N1, 2 and 3 representing progressively more extensive spread. The T and N categories are different for each cancer type and the definitions of those categories make up a substantial component of oncology text books and are beyond this text.

The "M" classification stands for metastases or spread to other distant organs. M0 is applicable where there is no such spread and M1 where there is a spread beyond the regional lymph nodes.

Sometimes, those categories are further subdivided using letters and numbers. An "x" tends to mean that no measurement can be taken. In addition, the insertion of a "p" before the letters TNM stands for pathological stage, whereas "c" stands for clinical stage. It follows from that analysis that cancers are often staged twice – first on a clinical basis. That assessment is an estimate of the extent of the cancer and is based upon clinical examination, radiology and biopsies. If surgery is then undertaken, a pathologic stage can be assessed upon the results of surgery and a histopathological analysis of the tissues removed. Those stages are not always the same.

Doubling Times

In the context of a claim dealing with a delay in cancer diagnosis, there is no clear basis upon which to assess the likely size of a tumour (or its spread) in the absence of a previous coincidental x-ray or scan on which the tumour was visible but missed as an incidental finding. That is a rare thing. As such, if there is no radiology or other screening lurking in the historic medical records of the client/patient, the retrospective staging of the tumour will depend upon a combination of data on average tumour growth rates (and which vary between types of cancers) and factors specific to the patient and the tumour's unique characteristics. We have already determined that each person's cancer is a unique creature and it follows from that, that there will undoubtedly be controversy in presenting evidence of averages as probative of injury in any particular claim.

Oncologists talk about doubling times or volume doubling times (VDT) to describe the likely growth of a cancer. The medical journals are littered with articles considering the variable (and of course average/mean) VDTs for different types of cancer. The medico legal oncology expert will no doubt base a large part of their view as to the likely growth rate of the claimant's cancer, and therefore the extent to which damage as a consequence of the alleged delay can be established, upon VDT literature.

The significance and management of the inevitable controversies surrounding VDTs will be considered in detail later on in this book, in the chapters dedicated to causation and expert evidence. However, a basic understanding of what is meant by doubling times and how they work is invaluable.

James J Stark, Professor of Medicine at the East Virginia Medical School, and author of the website starkoncology.com, describes doubling times in basic terms. Essentially, solid tumours (and so not blood borne tumours) have, as do most other solid items, three dimensions. If one knows or can work out the length, width and height of the primary tumour, one can then work out the average volume. The most accurate VDTs are therefore determined by considering the volume at two or more different moments in time. Therein lies the primary difficulty described above, where the volume is known or ascertainable at only one point in time.

The doubling time is then essentially the time taken for the tumour to double in volume (not in length, width or height). The calculations themselves are complex and beyond the scope of this book and its author's expertise, although there are online calculators available for use. It should also be borne in mind that metastases are generally faster growing than the primary tumour (Spratt et al J. Surg Oncol 61:68-83, 1996 by way of example).

The second difficulty with doubling times is the model upon which they are based. Some presuppose constant and predictable growth – such that if you have one cancer cell, it will double at every cell division, growing to two cells, then four, eight, sixteen and so on. However, research has shown that tumour growth is not constant or predictable over its life, but rather the growth rate slows with time. As such, the Gompertzian model of tumour growth developed by Laird AK in "Dynamics of tumour growth" Br J Cancer 1963; 18:490-502 assumes an exponentially decreasing growth rate over time and has become favoured in the assessment of cancer doubling times.

However, even the Gompertzian model has come under fire and there are other models out there to take account of the increasingly, but still incompletely understood means by which different tumours grow. The article by Philip Gerlee entitled "The Model Muddle: In Search of Tumour Growth Laws" published in April 2013 on cancerres.aacrjournals.org gives an interesting insight into the variety of and differences in modelling that exist and are probably unheard of in most legal claims relating to cancer diagnoses.

Summary

What have we established then?

- There is a rise in delayed cancer diagnosis litigation, due in part to a greater awareness of symptomatology and media coverage of the UK's poor performance alongside other countries when it comes to cancer survival rates.

- There is considerable variation in cancer survival rates depending upon region and socio-economic analysis.

- There are ongoing changes being made by the government in an attempt to improve the UK's survival rates and access to treatment. In particular, GP league tables started in 2013 and a voluntary audit commencing in September 2016 allow a review of how GP surgeries perform against national benchmarks, specifically in relation to the timing of referrals and diagnosis.

- Cancer is not one disease but a series of related diseases, each with its own unique fingerprint, and varying according to the patient's physiology and environmental factors.
- Cancer has the ability to invade surrounding structures and to spread through the blood and lymphatic systems.
- Whether cancer has spread is often only able to be determined by clinical assessment.
- Tumours and their spread / metastatic deposits take time to grow. There may be a period when either are not visible or detectable by any form of scanning.
- The treatment pathway and survival prospects are largely determined by the grade and stage of the cancer.
- The grade of the cancer does not change over time and may assist with assessing how likely the cancer is to spread, return or have a good or poor prognosis.
- There are various staging systems, of which the most used is the TNM system. There may be a difference between clinical and pathological staging.
- Where there is no previous x-ray or scan which shows the tumour and which is often absent in a delayed diagnosis claim, the likely stage of the tumour at any earlier date will probably be based in part upon a review of doubling times.
- The use of average doubling times is controversial (and will be considered further in relation to causation), and there is also controversy about the model for assessing VDTs.

- Most VDT models assume a degree of exponential growth or reduced growth over the life of the tumour. It is not however thought that tumours grow in a stepwise fashion.

CHAPTER THREE
THE OPENING REVIEW OF A CASE – USE OF GUIDELINES AND STATISTICS

This chapter will look at the first necessary steps in reviewing and investigating a potential delayed cancer diagnosis claim. In particular, it will consider how the NICE guidelines and other generic documents and statistics can be utilised in either:

(a) Building a case in respect of breach of duty for a claimant, or;

(b) Challenging such a claim for a defendant.

It will go on to consider practical ways of thinking outside the constraints of the language of the guidelines to provide novel opportunities for strengthening your client's case in respect of breach of duty.

It is plain that one cannot generally claim for getting cancer per se, save in specific limited occupational disease scenarios. The import of cancer claims in the clinical negligence setting is therefore in determining the difference that the correct or earlier diagnosis would have made to the patient's condition and prognosis. In real terms, these cases require the lawyer to strike a careful balance between two tricky timing issues. In most cases, the earlier the alleged date of negligence, at which point it is asserted that a diagnosis ought to have been reached, the harder it will be to establish a breach of duty but conversely, causation is likely to be more far reaching and easier to prove. On the other hand, the closer one gets to actual diagnosis, breach of duty is likely to become harder to defend, but equally, it will usually become harder to establish that any such breach of duty has made a material difference to the patient's outcome. The role of the lawyer is therefore to manage that conundrum and to find a way of maximising and balancing both breach of duty and causation. This chapter and those that follow aim to assist with finding a path through those complexities.

First Steps

Reviewing the medical records

In clinical negligence claims per se, but specifically in cancer claims, a thorough review of the medical records at an early stage is invaluable. The first step in early analysis of most cancer claims on either side, will be a non-expert look at the NICE guidelines (for which see below), and any pro-forma referral letters or documents utilised in the relevant region. That approach will generally be most informative if undertaken at the same time as a review of the complete medical records. If, as a claimant, time is of the essence due to the client's prognosis, attempts should be made through discussion with the proposed defendant and their lawyers to fast track the provision of records. Many defendant organisations are willing to assist with such requests in this type of claim.

There should be care taken to identify any missing records as soon as possible. There should also be careful examination and notation of:

(a) The number of visits reporting material symptoms;

(b) The quality of the medical notes at those consultations;

(c) The timeframe between visits, and in particular, the first visit and the claimant's ultimate diagnosis;

(d) The extent of any history taken and examination undertaken (including where the claimant is still alive a comparison between their own description of symptoms and background reported (including specific risk factors such as family history) and those recorded in the records);

(e) When referral took place and whether referral was urgent or routine. What information was provided on the referral letter?

(f) What if any, investigations were instigated in primary (and also in secondary) care, how quickly they took place, whether they were directly accessed, the speed with which they were followed up, and how they were followed up;

(g) What information was provided to the claimant/patient about their symptoms and the need for monitoring those symptoms (safety netting).

Given that the records can be extensive, it is often worth engaging a specialist company or in-house nursing staff to prepare a medical chronology and analysis of the records. That is not to say that such a step is justification for not undertaking a personal review of the documents, but they are often of great assistance when instructing experts, and in identifying any missing documents which need to be chased. Further, where the diagnosis or staging of a cancer is or is likely to be in any doubt, the histopathology samples should be obtained at the earliest opportunity for expert review.

Witness Evidence

The next critical step for the claimant lawyer is to obtain as detailed a witness statement as possible at the earliest stage, especially if the prognosis is poor. If at all possible the statement should be taken face to face rather than by telephone, and the client should, as always, be given the opportunity to explain in detail what they regard as important. Even if the client goes off at a tangent, an understanding of what they think has gone wrong can at least provide a useful basis for reviewing the records, instructing experts and undertaking broader investigation. The following checklist may sound painfully obvious but the foundations of the statement should include:

(a) Question number one – what specific type of cancer has the client been diagnosed with?

(b) What symptoms (and on how many occasions/over what timeframe) do they recall having reported to a medic?

(c) What information do they recall having given to the doctor(s) or treating medic(s) in relation to their symptoms, family history or other matters which they consider relevant?

(d) What treatment have they received so far and/or what treatment have they been advised to undergo?

(e) What prognosis have they been given?

With cancer claims, either where the client's prognosis is poor, or where the prognosis is not known and the client is undergoing treatment with its attendant uncertainties, the claimant lawyer may not have the luxury of time to take and then expand upon the statement at a later date. Nor may there, regrettably, be the opportunity to get the statement signed at a later date. Not only therefore should the statement be drafted early, but the claimant lawyer should also ensure that it (and each and every subsequent supplemental statement that may follow) is signed as soon as is practicable.

Of course, for a defendant, the need to take witness evidence is not so urgent. However, a brief statement from the key individuals as to what they recall of the material consultation(s), their assistance with the notes taken and the thinking behind them, and critically, the reasons for any actions taken and any decision not to refer at an earlier stage, together with an explanation for any apparent gaps (such as reference to the presence or absence of a family history of cancer or red flags) will still be useful in providing the groundwork for the investigation and assessment of prospects that must follow.

The NICE Guidelines

Most delayed cancer diagnosis claims start with the GP in primary care. The GP is generally the first port of call for the patient reporting symptoms which may be indicative of cancer and it is at this stage that delays are most likely to occur. It is the GP who usually suspects that a patient may be suffering from cancer. Secondary care providers are usually used to confirm or refute that suspicion by the administration of specific investigations. As such, the NICE guidelines for "Suspected Cancer: recognition and referral" are of both importance and assistance in evaluating any potential claim.

For more than a decade, NICE guidance has stated that patients who visit their family doctor with key signs of cancer should be referred to a specialist within two weeks. Those guidelines have been amended (most recently in 2015 (NG 12) to include a whole raft of additional symptoms worthy of investigation, and a recommendation that GPs are able to request some tests directly on an urgent basis, thus reflecting the increased availability of investigative aids in primary care and in general practise more broadly since the guidelines were implemented.

The most recent guidance is broad and far reaching. It covers around 35 cancer sites including but not limited to all of the most common sites, in addition to specific recommendations for children. The previous guidance was a decade old (Clinical Guideline [CG] 27, published in 2005), albeit with additional recommendations made in 2011. The new guidance followed years of debate but appears at least in part, to have been a response to the UK's performance statistics as described in the previous chapter.

NG 12 sets out two methods for organising their recommendations. The first is familiar from the 2005 guidance and structures recommendations by reference to cancer site, with symptoms and actions detailed thereunder. However, the subcategorization within each site heading (of which there are thirteen) is much more detailed than previously. In addition, there is a new heading for non-site specific symptoms. The 2015 guidelines also include a secondary method of organisation, namely by symptom and the findings of primary care investigations. That is eminently sensible because, of course, patients present not with a likely cancer and only with symptoms, some of which may be common to a variety of different cancer types.

The 2015 guidelines use a variety of terms to indicate the strength of the recommendations, ranging from "must" to "should" or "offer/consider". The meaning of those terms are set out as an appendix to the 2015 guidance. It states that:

> "*The Guideline Development Group makes a recommendation based on the trade-off between the benefits and harms of an intervention, taking into account the quality of the underpinning evidence. For some interventions, the Guideline Development Group is confident that, given the information it has looked at, most patients would choose the intervention. The wording used in the recommendations in this guideline denotes the certainty with which the recommendation is made....*"

"Must" is used to describe a legal duty to act or where the consequence of not acting would be extremely serious. "Should" is defined as a strong recommendation, where for the vast majority of patients, an intervention will do more good than harm, and be cost effective. Offer or consider are used when NICE are confident that an intervention will do more good than harm for most patients, and be cost effective, but other options may be similarly cost effective. The choice of intervention and whether or not to have the intervention at all in that scenario, is more likely to depend upon the patient's values and preferences than for a strong recommendation, and so the healthcare professional should spend more time considering and discussing options with the patient. Notably, NICE states that they only started to use this terminology in around 2009, such that the use of such terms, and specifically recommendations labelled with the term "consider" might not have the same meaning when considering the 2005 guidelines. Practitioners should therefore take care when interpreting the varying guidelines.

Both the 2005 and 2015 guidance go on to provide three main categories of referral: immediate, urgent and non-urgent. A further category of very urgent referral is included in the 2015 guidance. Immediate referral is required where symptoms are so bad that nothing but an immediate referral to hospital is adequate – defined as "*an acute admission or referral occurring within a few hours, or even more quickly if necessary*". Such cases are unlikely to be litigated as it is usually obvious where immediate referral is needed and causation would generally be extremely difficult to establish upon the back of any apparent breach. Non-urgent referrals are also less likely to be litigated as they tend to be used by GPs practising defensive medicine, and to exclude the potentially adverse diagnosis for reassurance and where cancer is unlikely.

Typically, urgent referrals are likely to be, and have routinely been, the most contentious area for litigation purposes. The guidelines define urgent referral as a two week referral. Very urgent referral is within 48 hours, and appears largely to be confined to childhood cancers and certain categories of brain and blood cancers.

It is also worth noting that, for the purposes of the guidance (both versions), "Unexplained" is defined as follows:

> "*Symptoms or signs that have not led to a diagnosis being made by the healthcare professional in primary care after initial assessment (including history, examination and any primary care investigations).*"

So how much reliance can we place upon the guidelines in establishing or defending breach of duty? The guidelines are expressed not to be mandatory. The overview section of the guidance expressly states as follows:

> "*The recommendations in this guideline represent the view of NICE, arrived at after careful consideration of the evidence available. When exercising their judgement, professionals and practitioners are expected to take this guideline fully into account, alongside the individual needs, preferences and values of their patients or the people using their service. It is not mandatory to apply the recommendations, and the guideline does not override the responsibility to make decisions appropriate to the circumstances of the individual, in consultation with them and their families and carers or guardian.*"

That having been said, the guidelines are also expressed to be independent, authoritative and evidence based. The processes and methods used are said to be in keeping with internationally accepted criteria of quality. The process by which the guidance is developed is intended to be based upon the best available evidence at the time with a view to effectiveness and cost, and the committees who make the recommendations are comprised of a collection of independent people, including lay members and healthcare professionals. They are generally taken to represent a consensus of views based upon common principles from published literature. As such, albeit not mandatory, it might be expected that they should be departed from only in exceptional circumstances.

In the case of ***Adshead v Tottle (2007) 25/10/2007 QBD LTL 21/1/2008,*** the claimant sought damages on behalf of the estate of his late wife. She had found a lump in her breast and went to her GP, the defendant. The defendant noted that she had a tender lump of 2cm diameter which she felt was benign. There was a factual dispute as to what safety netting advice Dr Tottle gave. In the event, Mrs Adshead, although returning to the surgery whilst pregnant in the intervening period, did not report any further issues with her breast until some fifteen months later, at which time a different GP found masses in both the breast and the axilla and made an urgent referral to the breast clinic. Mrs Adshead was diagnosed with breast cancer and underwent a mastectomy, radiotherapy and two courses of chemotherapy. However, her cancer was aggressive and she sadly died sixteen months after the diagnosis. She was just 35 years of age.

In terms of the factual judgement, Gray J concluded that Dr Tottle was negligent in not referring Mrs Adshead for urgent review, having found what he considered was a discrete breast lump. Further, the claimant's evidence as to what advice was given about follow up, and the fact that it was not made sufficiently clear to Mrs Adshead that she needed to return for a review, was accepted. It was further found that had she been referred urgently, Mrs Adshead's cancer would have been diagnosed four weeks later with surgery two weeks thereafter, giving rise to a 70% prospect of survival. It should be noted in respect of causation, that the judgement as to survival prospects followed a detailed analysis of the literature and the positive and negative prognostic factors in Mrs Adshead's case.

However, for present purposes, it is Gray J's comment as to the relevance of the NICE guidelines that is of interest. He noted that:

> "*I take Dr Budd's point that the guidelines are not prescriptive but it appears to me that, in circumstances such as obtained here, a failure on the part of a general practitioner to follow guidelines such as these*

> *is at least prima facie evidence of negligence on his or her part. I acknowledge that some of the other guidelines to which I was referred mention different ages than 30 as triggering the need for urgent referral. Most of those other guidelines post-date the consultation on 30th May 2000. It seems to me that the guidelines which are for present purposes the material ones are the Department of Health Guidelines which were in force at the time of the consultation."*

As such, Gray J's view was certainly that, whilst accepting that the guidelines (NICE or otherwise) are not mandatory, a failure to follow them would amount to prima facie evidence of negligence, and therefore presumably, would require cogent evidence to rebut it.

Similarly, in ***Ministry of Justice v Cheryl Carter (2010) EWCA Civ 694***, the claimant, who was a prisoner, visited the prison GP (three different doctors) on three occasions complaining of breast pain and a lump. On each occasion the breast was palpated but no lump felt. The claimant was later diagnosed with breast cancer following ultimate referral and proceeded to undergo mastectomy and chemotherapy. The claimant engaged Dr Ross, a GP expert, who stated that by the time of the third presentation, the GP should have become suspicious and made a referral (on a non-urgent basis because it was accepted that the examinations had all been undertaken non-negligently). Dr Cheng, GP engaged by the Trust, considered that where no lump was palpated, no referral was necessary. Expert oncology evidence established that at the time of the examinations in question it was unlikely that a lump would have been palpable. The Court of Appeal reversed the first instance judgement which found for the claimant and, they considered, failed properly to apply the Bolam test.

In that case, the applicable guidelines stated that where there was no palpable abnormality there was no evidence to support the use of mammography. Equally, a referral pro-forma issued by the relevant trust stated that women with moderate degrees of breast pain who do not have a discrete palpable lesion should have their initial care managed by a GP. The Court of Appeal noted that the guidelines included "*consultation with a very large body of interested professionals.*" It was further noted that in a preface to the Guidance by the Chairman of the Council of the Royal College of General Practitioners, it was suggested that whilst greater vigilance was needed, it was "*important not to routinely over-investigate or make inappropriate referrals*". The judge at first instance made no apparent reference to the guidelines.

It would therefore appear that in deciding between the divergent expert GP opinions, the Court of Appeal were, at least in part, swayed by the terminology and the status of the NICE guidelines in combination with the local referral pro-forma.

There is however some authority to suggest that a failure to follow the guidelines without more is not necessarily determinative of breach of duty. In ***Michael Mark Junior Darnley v Croydon Health Services NHS Trust (2015) Med LR 506***, the High Court (HHJ Robinson) considered a case in which the claimant had been attacked and struck on the head. He went to A&E, where he alleged that he was told by staff that he would be seen within four to five hours. The triage staff unsurprisingly had no recollection of the conversation but maintained that they would have told the claimant that he would be seen by a triage nurse within thirty minutes. He ultimately left the hospital nineteen minutes after he was booked in, without being treated, and later deteriorated. He was left with a left hemiplegia. The NICE clinical guidelines stated that a patient with a head injury should be assessed by a clinician within 15 minutes of arrival.

The case is better known for the finding that there was no general duty upon reception staff at a hospital to keep patients informed about likely waiting times, and nor was it fair, just and reasonable to establish a duty not to provide inaccurate information about waiting times. That decision was upheld by a majority of the Court of Appeal ***(2017) Med LR 245***. The Court of Appeal also considered that there was no basis for interfering with the High Court's judgement upon the facts, namely that Mr Darnley did not merit priority triage and/or that the failure to see him within fifteen minutes was not a breach of duty.

Paragraphs 37 to 62 of the High Court judgement of HHJ Robinson deal with the failure to comply with the NICE guidelines. Interestingly, in that case, the experts in their joint statements agreed that the standard of fifteen minutes to triage may not always be achievable depending upon clinical priorities and the level of activity within the department at the time. There was a degree of disagreement about the issue of a "triage within triage" system. The judge ultimately concluded that:

> "*The primary case of the claimant is straightforward and superficially attractive. The NICE guideline describes optimal practice. Anything less must represent sub-optimal practice and is therefore unacceptable....*
>
> *53. The real world position is not so simple, as was fairly recognised by Mr Heyworth when he qualified the evidence I have just quoted by saying: "We [the experts] agreed that up to 30 minutes may be the time allowable if there are adverse factors...*"
>
> *60. What I am prepared to find is that it seems to me to be extremely unlikely that the triage nurses were not fully engaged that night. The alleged breach of duty is a failure to meet a tight target of 15 minutes by a factor of 4 minutes. I am not prepared to find that this amounts to a breach of a clinical duty of care. It is right that there must be a longstop, or the target becomes meaningless. The consensus of opinion amongst the experts is that the longstop position is 30 minutes. That seems entirely appropriate....*"

The judge went on to find that even if there was a breach it was not causative of any loss, upon the basis that the damage arose due to the drastic deterioration in the claimant's condition after he chose to leave the hospital. He noted that the mischief which the guidelines were focused upon was the prevention of intra cranial damage.

What perhaps ought to be borne in mind is that the ***Darnley*** case above dealt with a very different set of circumstances than the average delayed cancer claim. The guidelines in question in that case were of a much tighter timeframe in the context of emergency hospital care. In most cancer claims where one is concerned with whether or not a referral for specialist investigation was undertaken, immediate time pressures and the practicalities of compliance will generally not exist. However, considerations of cost and resources no doubt will apply, although it may well be arguable that those features are already accounted for by the committee which set the recommendations and the terminology governing the strength of those recommendations in any event. However, what ***Darnley*** does highlight is that, regardless of the symptoms with which a patient presents and where they present, the guidelines are, as stated, not mandatory without more. There is seemingly, in an appropriate case, scope for defending breach of duty even where there has been a failure to comply with the guidelines, and which may be extremely useful to a defendant, depending upon the factual matrix of an alleged delayed diagnosis claim.

Against that background, it is notable that there are anecdotal reports of delayed cancer claims being increasingly defended upon the basis that departure from the NICE guidance does not amount to a breach of duty. It is in the nature of such claims, as with clinical negligence claims more generally, that the vast majority settle prior to trial. As such, there is, to the author's knowledge, no body of case law in recent years to record the views taken by the courts of such submissions. It therefore remains to be seen how, should an appropriate case make it to trial, a judge would look upon a defence of that nature.

How to Maximise Breach of Duty Submissions

I have already discussed above the need to undertake a close review of the guidelines and any pro-formas in conjunction with an early review of the medical records and a provisional witness statement. However, in light of the non-mandatory nature of the guidelines, how might claimants and defendants boost their respective positions when considering breach of duty (not accounting of course for the use of experts and which will be considered in greater detail in later chapters)?

Claimants may benefit from four additional approaches, although it remains to be seen how the courts would deal with such arguments in practise.

First, there may be some merit in relying as a secondary position upon the safety netting provisions within the NICE guidelines, and which have been subject to enhancement in the 2015 edition. Paragraph 1.15 of the 2015 guidelines provides as follows:

> "*1.15.1 Ensure that the results of investigations are reviewed and acted upon appropriately, with the healthcare professional who ordered the investigation taking or explicitly passing on responsibility for this. Be aware of the possibility of false-negative results for chest X-rays and tests for occult blood in faeces. [new 2015]*
>
> *1.15.2 Consider a review for people with any symptom that is associated with an increased risk of cancer, but who do not meet the criteria for referral or other investigative action. The review may be planned within a time frame agreed with the person or patient-initiated if new symptoms develop, the person continues to be concerned, or their symptoms recur, persist or worsen. [new 2015]*"

As such, consideration should be given, not just to whether there has been a referral, especially where the symptoms presented with may be on the cusp of justifying referral or may otherwise not be sufficient at that stage for referral, but also whether, if the symptom is "associated with an increased risk of cancer" an appropriate review has been arranged.

Secondly, paragraph 1.16 provides advice in relation to the process of diagnosis. Paragraph 1.16.2 indicates that:

> "*Discussion with a specialist (for example, by telephone or email) should be considered if there is uncertainty about the interpretation of symptoms and signs, and whether a referral is needed. This may also enable the primary healthcare professional to communicate their concerns and a sense of urgency to secondary healthcare professionals when symptoms are not classical.*"

Consequently, if, as frequently happens, the defence position is that the claimant's symptoms were unusual in presentation, or that there were differing acceptable interpretations to be placed upon the claimant's presentation, it could be argued that rather than settling upon an alternative benign diagnosis, a defendant GP ought to have obtained a second opinion by means of discussion with a specialist. It is unclear precisely when the guideline at Paragraph 1.16.2 is intended to apply, and quite how uncertain the interpretation of symptom would need to be before requiring further action. It is no doubt arguable that most symptoms may be interpreted in different ways. However, it would surprising if discussion with a specialist were to be required on every such occasion. To do so would plainly be inefficient, costly and unworkable.

The remainder of Paragraph 1.16 goes on to ensure that all relevant information is included in any referral form, including the urgency of the referral (which should always be checked), as well as whether appropriate local arrangements are in place for maximum waiting times and the follow up of patients who miss appointments. There are largely comparable provisions in the 2005 guidelines with some minor variations, although paragraphs 1.15.1. and 1.15.2 are both new to the 2015 guidelines. That having been said, Paragraphs 1.2.2 and 1.2.3 of the 2005 guidelines provide for some, albeit less stringent or regulated form of review.

Thirdly, in an appropriate case, one should consider whether there may be a consent or information concern. Paragraphs 1.14.1 – 1.14.11 of the 2015 guidelines provide helpful details about what information and support should be provided to patients, and paragraphs 1.14.5 and 1.14.9 may be particularly relevant. It should be noted that in the recent case of ***Raul Guiu Gallardo v Imperial College Healthcare NHS Trust (2018) PIQR P6,*** Judge Peter Hughes QC, sitting in the High Court, was concerned with a case in which the claimant, who was Spanish, had required major abdominal surgery in January 2001 following a CT scan which had revealed a stomach mass. A malignant tumour was removed and the claimant had a stormy postoperative course, after which he was discharged in April 2001. During the course of his recovery he was transferred prior to discharge, to a private ward. He was for a time too ill for discussions to take place. He began to experience stomach pain again in 2006 and self-referred to a specialist cancer hospital after a number of unsatisfactory diagnoses, as a result of which contact was made with the claimant's previous surgeon. In an email response to the claimant in November 2010, the surgeon advised that the surgery in 2001 had removed a malignant gastrointestinal stromal tumour which carried a risk of recurrence. He ultimately had complex surgery in 2011 and further surgery was likely to be required. The experts agreed that the claimant should have been advised to undergo regular CT scans, which, had they been performed would have led to the tumour being identified and operated upon in 2006, at a time when it would have been smaller.

It was held that there were no records of any discussions regarding treatment and prognosis prior to his internal transfer or ultimate hospital discharge. The discharge letter referred to the tumour by a different name. The letter to the claimant's GP referred to the tumour as malignant but not to the need for regular follow up. The judge concluded that it was a patient's right to be informed of the outcome of any treatment, the prognosis, and the options for follow-up care and treatment. Information should only be withheld in exceptional circumstances, and for clear and persuasive therapeutic reasons. However, the timing of those discussions depended upon a variety of factors. The discussion should have occurred as soon as the claimant was well enough to participate in the discussion and should not be delayed on therapeutic grounds unless there would be serious detriment to the patient's health. As such ***Montgomery v Lanarkshire Health Board (2015) 2 WLR 768***, applied.

Whilst it might be anticipated that those circumstances will be few and far between, there may be rather more subtle issues of consent which a claimant might seek to rely upon in appropriate circumstances.

Finally, one means of underpinning a guideline indicative of a need to refer a patient, may be to garner evidence in support of the premise upon which the guidelines are based. The 2015 guidelines use a risk of cancer (or a positive predictive value/PPV) of 3% or more to underpin the recommendation for urgent referral or further investigation. There are a few exceptions, principally in relation to children and young people when a lower PPV is utilised. The overview to the guidelines makes clear that the 2005 guidelines used a range of percentages but with few below a PPV of 5%. As such, the 2015 guidelines are generally more stringent.

Consequently, if there is likely to be argument about whether a failure to follow the guidelines constitutes a breach of duty, there may be some merit in inviting one's experts to provide specific information about the positive predictive value or the risk of cancer attributable to the particular claimant's symptoms and circumstances, and specifically the values associated with circumstances such as age, family history, smoking history (in lung and pleural cancers), a history of sun exposure perhaps (in skin cancer cases), and maybe even socio-economic factors based upon geographical location and quality of life. Whilst the author is unaware of these background factors being relied upon or considered in any reported case, there may well be greater likelihood of securing a finding of breach of duty if the guideline has not been followed and one can show that the PPV attributable to the claimant's presentation and underlying circumstances exceeds 3% (or 5% if referable to the 2005 guidelines), preferably by some margin.

For defendants, plainly consideration of the positive predictive values may be of equal value in supporting a defence position if the PPV can be shown to be either below or on the cusp of the underlying 3% or 5% thresholds. Similarly, if steps can be shown to have been taken to arrange a review, provide suitable information and safety netting advice, those factors may assist in strengthening a defence to the effect that a failure to follow the letter of the guidance does not amount to a breach of duty.

A key factor in defending delayed cancer diagnosis claims may well be the ability to rely upon a symptom presentation which, whilst potentially within the symptom cluster for cancer, is also present within a range of benign conditions. The following chapter will look more closely at the impact of different cancer types upon the strength of a claim for delay.

However, one area which may be worth pursuing, depending upon the timeframe in question is the extent to which the NICE guidance may have changed. Of course, the standard of care in any one case depends upon compliance with a responsible body of expert opinion at the material time (since the time of ***Bolam***). So, for example, if a claimant complains of a failure to refer her for urgent investigation for breast cancer at an appointment or series of appointments in 2007, the issue of breach will turn upon the standards in place (and therefore be informed by the guidance in placed) in 2007. So far as the NICE guidance is concerned, the 2005 CG27 guidelines would be applicable, rather than the 2015 (NG12) guidance,

Further, because of the fact that the requirement to apply the state of knowledge at the material, time prevents doctors being penalised for failing to apply knowledge which had yet to be acquired, it would appear likely to be much more difficult for claimants to rely upon positive changes leading to more stringent requirements as between say, the 2005 and 2015 guidelines as indicative of breach of duty when dealing with historic claims prior to the implementation of the latter document without cogent evidence. That having been said, both claimant and defendant should ensure that their experts consider and provide evidence to support the state of knowledge more generally at the point of any alleged negligence. It is notable that, for example, even though the guidelines may only have been published in, say, 2005 or 2015, the knowledge of the matters within them may well have been commonly held for some time (and sometimes years) prior to their publication.

Notwithstanding the transitional state of knowledge prior to the publication of later guidelines, what of the occasional situation where the guidelines might have, or appear to have become less stringent with time, or are now silent upon a once apparently mandatory provision?

In the case of ***Adshead v Tottle (2007) 25/10/2007 QBD LTL 21/1/2008*** referred to above, Gray J also commented at paragraph 39 that:

> *"It is in my opinion nothing to the point that the guidelines may have altered at a later date. This is not a case where there is room for the application of the Bolam principle. In the case of a patient who presents with a potentially life-threatening symptom, I do not accept*

that a responsible general practitioner would delay referring her, even for a short period, in circumstances where the recommendation made unambiguously in the guidelines is to refer immediately."

That may well be regarded as a death blow for an argument that a downgrading of the guidelines at a later date is irrelevant to the court's determination. However, it may be arguable that the matters with which Gray J was concerned in ***Adshead*** were rather different.

As an example, let us consider the guidance in relation to lung cancer. The 2005 guidelines provided as follows:

"*1.3.2 An urgent referral for a chest X-ray should be made when a patient presents with:*

- *haemoptysis, or*

- *any of the following unexplained persistent (that is, lasting more than 3 weeks) symptoms and signs....*"

There have been some positive changes in the 2015 guidance when compared with 2005 in that there is now a requirement for a chest x ray to be undertaken within two weeks in people older than 40 and with either two unexplained symptoms if they have never smoked or one if they are a smoker, with those symptoms being taken from a defined list. There is also now a recommendation that those over 40 reporting "*unexplained haemoptysis*" should be referred urgently under the two-week pathway for specialist investigation. The definition of "*unexplained*" set out earlier should be borne in mind. Those changes accord with greater knowledge of increased risk acquired over time.

It is apparent from a simple comparison that the urgency attributed to unexplained haemoptysis appears to have increased, with a requirement for immediate urgent referral without recourse to an x-ray. However, it may be thought that the 2005 guidance suggested that an urgent referral for a chest x-ray was required for a patient of any age presenting with <u>any</u> episode of haemoptysis, even if isolated and small in quantity. The 2015 guidance does not appear to recommend a chest x-ray at all for a patient presenting with haemoptysis, unless their haemoptysis is unexplained (which would seem to suggest a degree of recurrence) and in which case they would proceed straight to a cancer referral.

Might it therefore be possible for a defendant in a case where a claimant presenting prior to 2015 with limited or apparently explained haemoptysis, who later turns out to have lung cancer which would have been identified on a plain chest x-ray, to claim that the apparent down-playing of the guidance surrounding haemoptysis in 2015 ought to inform whether a failure to refer the patient for a chest x-ray earlier amounts to a breach of duty? That has yet to be seen but defendants may well seek to enhance their defence in appropriate cases based upon those types of changes.

Finally, let us not forget the league tables and the voluntary audit data referred to in Chapter two above. Whilst evidence of generic poor performance by a GP practise as a whole, and which will encompass the practises of numerous partners cannot be probative, not to mention the issues with interpreting the records alluded to earlier in this book, claimants and defendants may well wish (and be well advised) to add impetus to their claims (and the prospects of negotiation) by considering how the GP practise with which any claim is concerned, has performed against local and national benchmarks, and whether any trends can be identified (positive or negative) with regard to suspected cancer referral timeframes.

Summary

- A thorough review of the medical records at an early stage is invaluable. Try to arrange for records to be fast tracked if time is of the essence or there is concern about life expectancy.

- Consider getting a specialist company to undertake a records chronology and be sure to identify missing records as soon as possible.

- Have a checklist of queries set out when considering the records and the critical appointments at which the claimant has presented with the symptoms which are said to be indicative of cancer. Consider also the quality of the notes, and identification of (or notation of having asked about) red flags/family history etc:

- Review the records in conjunction with a non-expert review of the NICE guidelines for the specific type of cancer with which the claimant has since been diagnosed.

- For Claimants, obtain as detailed a witness statement as possible at the earliest stage, especially if the prognosis is poor and get it signed.

- Most delayed cancer diagnosis claims start with the GP in primary care.

- The first port of call for assessing the GPs actions will usually be the Suspected Cancer: recognition and referral NICE guidance, the most recent version of which is NG12 (2015). The previous version was CG27 in 2005.

- The 2015 guidelines are organised both by cancer type and by symptom.

- The guidelines use a variety of terms to indicate the strength of the recommendations. They also provide for four categories of referral of which "urgent" is the most likely to be litigated.

- The guidelines are expressed to be non-mandatory but are generally regarded as independent, authoritative and evidence based. There is case law to suggest that a departure from the guidance will be prima facie evidence of negligence.

- There is however also some authority to suggest that a failure to follow the guidelines without more is not necessarily determinative of breach of duty.

- Claimants may benefit from relying also upon the safety netting provisions within the guidelines.

- Equally, consideration should be given to whether symptoms are of unusual presentation or allow for different interpretations so as to invoke a requirement to seek specialist advice by email or telephone.

- Consider also whether there are any consent/information breaches.

- Try to obtain evidence of the positive predictive values in respect of the claimant's symptoms and circumstances and consider whether they are below or above the percentage PPV underlying the relevant NICE guidance.

- Consider the extent to which the guidance has changed as between different versions of the guidance and whether an argument can be formulated to take advantage of those changes (usually for defendants).

- Do not forget to assess (with one's experts) when the knowledge underlying the revised (and often more stringent guidelines) was first commonly known about within the professional arena.

- Consider evidence from the league tales and GP audits.

CHAPTER FOUR
DIFFERENT TYPES OF CANCER AND THEIR VARIED LEGAL IMPACT

This chapter will consider whether and the extent to which the type of cancer diagnosed has a bearing upon the ease or otherwise of establishing breach of duty and/or causation. It aims to provide the practitioner with a grounding in the array of cancer types which exist and how that can be transposed into the legal setting, as well as helping to identify at an early stage which types of claim are likely to require additional steps to get and keep them on track.

Multiple Consultations

So far as breach of duty is concerned, the same principles apply across the board, and regardless of which subtype of cancer one is dealing with.

However, it is likely that the difficulties of establishing a breach of duty specifically in relation to the timing of ultimate diagnosis, do vary with the type of cancer concerned.

As considered in previous chapters, it must be remembered that cancer is a highly heterogenous disease. National audit and patient survey data appear to show that the strongest predictor of multiple consultations (and which in turn increase the time from presentation to referral and diagnosis) is tumour site.

The audits and surveys referred to earlier in this book include data (albeit with the limitations identified previously) upon the average number of consultations which patients routinely attend between initial presentation and diagnosis. The data are focused upon identifying which cancers have the greatest potential and/or need for improvement in speed of referral, to address the concerns raised regarding delay in diagnosis and survival rates. However, they can also help legal professionals to identify where problems may lie for claimants in the management of delayed diagnosis claims, or alternatively, a means of defending a claim for defendants.

An article in the Lancet entitled "*Variation in number of general practitioner consultations before hospital referral for cancer: findings from the 2010 National Cancer Patient Experience Survey in England*" by Dr Georgios Lyratzopoulos, Richard Neal, Josephine Barbiere, Professor Rubin and Gary Abel, Lancet Oncol2012; 13:353-65, set about analysing data from 41, 299 patients with 24 different cancers who took part in the 2010 Survey. They concluded that there was significant variation as between cancer type in the numbers of patients who had visited their GP at least three times prior to a referral being made. For example, only 7·4% of patients surveyed for breast cancer and 10·1% for melanoma had undergone multiple consultations pre-referral. Patients with testicular and endometrial cancer also had fewer consultations. By contrast, 41·3% of patients ultimately diagnosed with pancreatic cancer and 50·6% of those with multiple myeloma were seen on more than three occasions by their GP. Patients with stomach cancer and lung cancer also had higher numbers of consultations.

The University of Cambridge research website, considering the data which formed the basis of that article, quotes Dr Lyratzopoulos, the lead investigator as saying:

> "*These findings highlight limitations in current scientific knowledge about these cancers…Medical research in recent decades has prioritised improving cancer treatments, but knowledge about the 'symptom signature' of common cancers and practical solutions on how best to diagnose them is still emerging….*"

Another article by Abel, Lyratzopoulos and others titled "*Emergency diagnosis of cancer and previous general practice consultations: insights from linked patient survey data*" Br J Gen Pract. 2017 Jun; 67(659): e377–e387, is interesting. The article's focus is slightly different, in that it considered how many patients with cancer diagnosed as emergencies, had had previous consultations with their GP complaining of relevant symptoms, and of those how many had multiple consultations. The article concluded that of 4,647 emergency patients, 29% surprisingly reported no prior consultations, with the highest numbers for those with brain cancer and the lowest for those with mesothelioma. Of 3,298 emergency patients with prior consultations, some 41% had already had at least three consultations.

An extremely useful results table (table 2) within the article compiles a list of cancers by site and which identified the proportions of patients with more than one and then with more than three prior GP consultations. As before, multiple myeloma and non-Hodgkin's lymphoma top the board, with mesothelioma, breast cancer and leukaemia at the bottom.

Why Are Some Cancers More Likely to Require Multiple Consultations?

In yet another article by the very prolific Dr Lyratzopoulos, Greg Rubin and Jane Wardle, "*Rethinking diagnostic delay in cancer: how difficult is the diagnosis?*" BMJ 2014; 349:g7400, the authors consider the reasons behind these variations. They reiterate that around 50% of patients subsequently diagnosed with cancer are referred to a hospital specialist after one consultation, with a further 30% being referred after two consultations. The remaining 20% wait rather longer. National audit data are reported to show that after three consultations, the median time to referral is 34 days. That increases to 47 days after four appointments and 96 days for five or more. However, the article goes on to say that many patients have even longer wait times, with some 25% of those visiting a GP three, four and five or more times waiting longer than 64, 90, and 172 days, respectively.

They went on to consider whether cancers could be classified by difficulty in diagnosis. Cancers were classed as either harder to suspect (those presenting with non-specific symptoms), intermediate (some of whom present with specific symptoms and some presenting with atypical features) and those which are easier to suspect (most presenting with highly specific symptoms or signs). Examples of which types of cancer may fall within each bracket are identified as following the previously described tables according to multiple consultation status.

The diagnostic difficulty categorisation and in turn the tendency towards multiple consultations for those in the harder to diagnose category appear to reflect the cluster of symptoms with which those cancers present.

For example, patients with breast cancer tend to present with specific symptoms, most notably a palpable breast lump, or in some cases with nipple discharge or retraction. Similarly, those with skin cancer tend to present with a visible lesion to the skin which is assessed according to a weighted checklist of factors determined to identify the degree of suspicion to be held. One would naturally expect those types of cancer to require only one or at most two consultations before a referral is made.

Conversely, the harder to diagnose category of cancers frequently present either with atypical features, with symptoms which mimic other conditions or with a set of symptoms which are extremely common in a range of benign and common ailments. Take multiple myeloma as an example. In an article by Dean Smith and Kwee Yong titled "*Multiple Myeloma*" BMJ 2013; 346: f3863, it is noted that presenting symptoms are often non-specific and may include fatigue and back pain. They noted that one report indicated that some 56% of patients presenting to their GP then wait more than six months to see a haematologist with a third of cases being diagnosed through the emergency route and suffering poorer outcomes. It need barely be stated that fatigue and back pain are perhaps two of the most common symptoms with which patients suffering entirely benign conditions present to their GP. The National Institute for Neurological Disorders and Stroke reports on their website that around 80% of adults experience low back pain at some point in their lives with it being the most common cause of job-related disability. They state that more than a quarter of adults reported experiencing low back pain during the previous three months. Similarly, www.patient.info/doctor reports that 5-7% of patients attend their GP with a primary complaint of fatigue. We live increasingly stressful lives and work increasingly long hours, so that fatigue is, to a degree, to be expected as part of normal life.

For similar reasons, many head and neck cancers present with symptoms such as a sore throat or blocked nose. NHS UK's website confirms that the symptoms of nose and sinus cancer in particular, are similar to viral or bacterial infections such as the common cold or sinusitis. Pancreatic cancer, another hard to diagnose cancer, frequently presents in its earlier stages with symptoms such as abdominal and back pain and indigestion. This, according to www.Pancreaticcancer.org.uk makes it difficult to spot.

It is perhaps telling that the easier to diagnose cancers have comparatively small sections within the aforementioned NICE guidelines, whereas those that are rather more difficult, take up comparatively more space and are peppered with a requirement that symptoms be "persistent" and/or "unexplained".

How Does This Affect Breach of Duty?

Often, it will follow from such presentations that in the absence of red flag symptoms or a strong family history, conservative treatments for routine conditions, allied with a watch and see approach, will be justified. There may also be a higher incidence of investigations undertaken in primary care, which then need to return, and be followed up, before referral occurs.

The reality is that, if the cancer with which the Claimant is ultimately diagnosed is of a type generally regarded as easier to diagnose and presenting with more specific symptoms, one would expect the records to reflect only one or perhaps two consultations prior to specialist referral and diagnosis. If the records conversely reflect a higher than average number of consultations in respect of those symptoms, then, absent any atypical features, it may be anticipated that breach of duty will be easier to establish. Similarly, it will frequently be rather harder for Claimants to establish that multiple consultations without a diagnosis being reached is indicative of negligence where the cancer type in question is in the harder to suspect category with a more generalised presentation.

Those differences in signature symptoms and the consequent increase in the reasonable period of time between presentation and referral, will often have a knock-on effect upon causation, which is considered further below.

That having been said, the issue for the lawyer will be to gauge the point at which the balance between reasonable conservative treatment and monitoring and concern at the prospect of a more sinister cause, tips in favour of the latter and mandates onward referral or further investigation.

Those considerations will require careful examination with one's experts, backed where possible by literature and statistical data. It will also often be all the more important in such claims, to keep in mind the following issues and whether breach of duty may be established on an alternative basis:

(a) Whether sufficient monitoring has been implemented and whether a review of the Claimant's symptoms has been suitably fixed or left for the Claimant to instigate after effective consultation;

(b) Whether and at what point, symptoms are sufficiently uncertain to require discussion with a specialist pursuant to the 2015 NICE guidance at paragraph 1.16;

(c) Whether and to what extent (if the 2015 guidelines apply), the guidelines dealing with non-site-specific guidelines or those based upon symptom rather than cancer type are more helpful.

Summary

- It is likely that the difficulties of establishing a breach of duty specifically in relation to the timing of ultimate diagnosis, do vary with the type of cancer concerned.

- National audit and patient survey data appear to show that the strongest predictor of multiple consultations is tumour site.

- Data appears to indicate that there is significant variation as between cancer type in the numbers of patients who had visited their GP at least three times prior to a referral being made.

- Multiple myeloma and non-Hodgkin's lymphoma tend to require a greater number of consultations prior to diagnosis, whereas mesothelioma, breast cancer and leukaemia are shown to have the fewest.

- Cancers have in some articles, been classed as either harder to suspect (those presenting with non-specific symptoms), intermediate (some of whom present with specific symptoms and some presenting with atypical features) and those which are easier to suspect (most presenting with highly specific symptoms or signs).

- That categorisation appears to reflect the cluster of symptoms with which those cancers present.

- The harder to diagnose category of cancers frequently present either with atypical features, with symptoms which mimic other conditions or with a set of symptoms which are extremely common in a range of benign and common ailments.

- It may be that in the absence of red flag symptoms or a strong family history, conservative treatments for routine conditions, allied with a watch and see approach, will be justified more frequently in the harder to diagnosis category cancers and that breach of duty will be harder to establish.

- Greater emphasis may therefore need to be put upon whether sufficient monitoring, review and/or discussion surrounding uncertain symptoms has been put in place.

CHAPTER FIVE
EXPERTS

This chapter will consider how the lawyer should go about finding and instructing experts in delayed cancer diagnosis claims. It aims to provide the practitioner with tools which, as well as being, in some respects, of universal application to all cases in which expert witnesses have to be instructed, will allow an early and more tailored approach to be taken to such evidence in complex cancer claims.

Expert Selection

Once one has undertaken the initial review of the claim, taken an early witness statement, obtained the records and reviewed them alongside the applicable guidelines and pro-formas, the next step is usually to set about identifying and instructing suitable experts.

Expert selection is critical in most cases, whether dealing with cancer or otherwise. There is, in such circumstances, nothing more reliable than personal (preferably recent) experience of an expert, both on paper and in court as the best means of choosing one's expert. Failing that, asking for the recommendations of colleagues can be invaluable. It is imperative that credible experts are used, and it is therefore always worth trawling recent cases (on Lawtel for example) dealing with cancer claims to ascertain which experts have been commended, and found persuasive by the court (specifically in a case dealing with the particular type of cancer with which one is concerned) and perhaps even more importantly, which have been discredited or found wanting. It is as important if not more important to ascertain which experts not to use as which to trust with your instructions. Once initial experts have been selected, they may also be able to assist in recommending additional experts in due course.

It is also useful to instruct teams of experts who have a track record of working well together, and where possible, to avoid instructing experts who are known to have either a personality clash or an acrimonious professional relationship with one's other expert witnesses. Just as the treatment of cancer in scientific terms is dealt with on a multi -disciplinary team basis, so too is it important that the individuals involved in the management of a cancer claim, including the crucial expert witnesses, gel as a team.

The Right Experts?

It is usually worth only instructing an expert on the liability aspects of the case in the first instance, so as to save costs, and help to set the parameters for further experts. However, one has to know also that the claimant had cancer which was detectable at the alleged date of negligence as plainly, no claim can be sustained upon the basis of a failure to refer for, say, a breast lump which was in fact benign.

As such, both claimant and defendant lawyers are likely to require expert evidence regarding whether the cancer found at ultimate diagnosis was present and detectable at the alleged date of negligence and so, there will generally be a need for two experts in respect of breach alone, one of which will usually be an oncologist. Plainly, the specialism(s) of the liability expert(s) will be determined by the nature of the failures initially alleged. It is anticipated that (as considered above) the vast majority of delayed cancer diagnosis claims will at least in part, focus upon primary care and require expert evidence from a GP. If there are additional allegations which appear to arise from the records, such as a failure to report x-rays or scans correctly, or instituting an inappropriate treatment regime, liability reports may also then be required from a radiologist and/or an oncologist.

Moreover, if, upon initial review of the records and guidelines, the lawyer takes the view that breach of duty appears provisionally strong but that causation is likely to be the most difficult aspect of the claim, it may be most sensible to obtain causation evidence first, before incurring the costs of investigating breach of duty. It is of little use establishing a breach of duty if your client will inevitably fall at the hurdle of causation. Such decisions can only be made on a common sense basis.

The starting point for dealing with causation in any cancer claim, and therefore to assessing which experts are required, is to assess the correct team responsible for the claimant's care, and to ascertain who would have had responsibility for what. Over 95% of cancer cases will be discussed at an appropriately appointed multi-disciplinary team meeting (MDT). The make-up of the MDT will depend upon the type of cancer.

For example, an MDT for lung cancer will generally include the following (as provided for in numerous hospital/NHS trust websites and as follows, by the National Lung Cancer Forum for Nurses):

- Chest / Respiratory physician – They undertake tests such as chest x-rays and/or bronchoscopies to aid in diagnosing lung cancer. They are often also the professional with responsibility for co-ordinating the cancer pathway.

- Oncologist- They typically deal with the non-surgical treatment of cancer (ie: chemotherapy and radiotherapy).

- Lung Cancer Nurse Specialist (LCNS) – The provider of specialist lung cancer information/ support to patients and their families.

- Thoracic Surgeon – They generally undertake chest surgery, including excision of the lung and symptom management.

- Radiologist - Undertakes radiological investigations including x-rays, CT scans, PET, MRI and bone scans.

- Histopathologist – Responsible for reviewing biopsy and other samples to determine the type of cancer

- Palliative Care Team – Responsible for symptoms management (usually where the cancer cannot be cured).

For bowel cancer, the MDT will typically include the following:

- Colorectal surgeon

- Oncologist
- Clinical Nurse Specialist
- Radiologist
- Histopathologist
- Gastroenterologist
- Palliative care team

In causative terms, expert evidence from a nursing or palliative care specialist is usually not required (unless of course there are allegations of breach dealing with nursing, which are themselves infrequent and also unlikely in most cases to have caused additional injury). However, expert evidence will generally be needed from:

(a) An oncologist;

(b) A radiologist and;

(c) The specialist surgeon/physician.

In lung cancer cases, a chest physician will also generally be required to comment upon the patient's likely diagnosis and treatment management, as well as life expectancy.

Psychologists and others may well also be involved in due course. In head and neck cancers, speech and language therapists and dieticians will frequently be involved in a patient's care. In breast cancer (and other cancers such as skin cancer, some head and neck cancers etc:), reconstructive plastic surgeons will also likely be involved. Such specialisms are usually more relevant to a subsequent assessment of loss and damage rather than causation.

Primary first stage causation evidence will almost always be required from the oncologist as to the grade, staging, growth rate/doubling time and prognosis for the cancer at different time points within the case.

Once the staging and size of the tumour is assessed, a report will generally be needed from a radiologist to identify the extent to which a tumour of the size supported by one's oncologist or other expert, would have been visible on a plain x-ray and/or a CT scan (or whatever form of investigation the experts assert should have been undertaken) so as to have mandated further action being taken. They will also be able to advise upon the appearances of any scans obtained and the accuracy of the radiology reports throughout the history of the diagnostic process. Thereafter, one is also likely to require a surgical opinion (again specific to the particular type of cancer with which you are dealing) to address (in combination with the oncologist) what treatment the Claimant would likely have been offered and with what likely outcome. Histopathology evidence is likely to be required if there is an issue as to the type of cancer in question, which was the primary and which the secondary tumour, and /or the grade and composition of the tumour at issue.

Consequently, whilst a review of the MDT cannot of course, tell the lawyer which experts to instruct and which to leave aside, it is a useful checklist to identify which specialisms may be relevant to a particular case, what they can assist with, and potentially, in which order, especially with less common forms of the disease. Most hospital trusts will have a page documenting the MDT in clear language aimed at patients, for each cancer type. As such, if in any doubt, the MDT configuration can be identified with ease through any basic internet search.

Instructing the Experts

It cannot be overstated how important it is, when instructing experts, to ensure efficient planning. That is true of any claim but none more so than the delayed cancer diagnosis claim given their multiple complexities.

In order to instruct one's experts, the lawyer must first have a clear grasp upon what is required and what the preliminary case is. The author appreciates that for the vast majority of experienced practitioners, the basics of instructing experts are second nature. However, for those who are new to this field, and even for more experienced practitioners, it is never a mistake occasionally to check that the basics are not being forgotten in the quest for detail.

As such, before embarking upon any expert instruction, especially in this type of case, the practitioner (whether claimant or defendant focused) may well benefit from compiling a bullet point list for both breach of duty and causation, identifying each of the key factual and legal issues that the claimant would need to establish in order to succeed in their claim. Cancer cases in particular require a methodical and structured approach. Not only will a clear and concise document identifying the issues help with the structure of one's instructions, but will also:

(a) Hopefully assist the expert in structuring their report in an easy to follow and lay client/lawyer friendly manner, and;

(b) Serve as a useful checklist for the practitioner upon receipt of the report(s) in assessing whether there are any obvious gaps in the evidence obtained that need to be remedied.

Once the background preparation is complete, one must obviously start by making it clear whether the expert is being asked to report upon liability and/or causation or condition and prognosis or both. The instructions should go on to set out and enclose the following:

(a) A clear copy of all of the medical records, organised logically and in clearly distinguished sections (ie: GP records, records from specific hospitals or alternatively organised chronologically within sections for specific timeframes, radiotherapy records, pathology, radiology, drug charts etc).

(b) The documents should be clearly paginated without any sections excised during the photocopying process!

(c) If there are documents which have not been obtained or where problems lie in their retrieval, inform the expert in the instruction letter together with an indication as to what steps are being taken to obtain them and any expected timeframe.

(d) The documents provided should be listed in an index at the start of the instructions and one should ask the expert to confirm that they have received all of the enclosures and to inform you as soon as possible if they consider any documents to be missing.

(e) A chronology prepared either by the lawyer or by a specialist agency reviewing the records, should be included with the instructions as an aid.

(f) The expert should also be sent a clear and concise statement of the client's (whether that be the claimant, the deceased claimant's nearest and dearest or the defendant medic(s)) version of events and key complaints or disputes of fact). Where possible, any obvious discrepancies between that version of events and the records should be highlighted. For obvious reasons, the lawyer may not wish to send the expert a copy of the client's early statement, or for the expert to refer to the same in their report. However, the information contained within any such statement will need to be provided in an appropriate form.

(g) The expert should be asked specifically to address any concerns regarding inconsistency between the statement and the records and to address how that might affect their view. Where there are obvious discrepancies, they should be asked in clear terms to provide their opinion based upon both versions of events.

(h) The instructions must then, as always, contain a succinct but accurate summary of the key facts as the client and lawyer understand them, the preliminary issues identified and the key legal tests to be applied.

(i) As a backstop, the instructions must always ask the expert to comment upon any matters not highlighted which they consider to be relevant.

Thereafter, perhaps the most difficult aspect of the expert's instructions but equally one of the most important, is to set out a clear list of questions for the expert to address (subject as above to the caveat that anything else they consider to be relevant should also be included). It is in the formation of the questions that preparation and a thoughtful approach to the issues in logical order, is paramount.

It is best to begin with general questions and then more specific questions which are phrased in an open ended format to encourage thorough and unbiased answers. By way of example, when instructing a causation (usually oncology) expert in a cancer claim, general questions may include things like:

(a) Please discuss what outcome would have been expected on the balance of probabilities, but for the negligence.

(b) Describe how that outcome compares with the patient's actual outcome. In other words, on balance how has the alleged negligence altered the clinical outcome?

(c) If there has been a negligent delay in treatment and if you have not already done so, please consider whether and to what extent that delay has affected the client's clinical outcome.

More specific questions may include:

(a) Describe the precise form of cancer which the patient has acquired, as confirmed by histopathological diagnosis;

(b) Explain the expected natural history of that type of cancer. In so doing, please address;

(c) How long and well do people live with it?

(d) What is the likely doubling time or growth rate?

(e) Are there any concerns about using doubling times or growth rates and are there any features of this cancer or patient which affect you view?

(f) Is it likely that the cancer is amenable to screening – what is the duration of its detectable pre-clinical phase?

(g) On the balance of probabilities, how advanced or widespread was the cancer at the time when the alleged negligence occurred (ie: what were its likely dimensions, is it likely to have metastasised, was there likely nodal involvement?)

And the list goes on! The expert should be asked to provide literature where possible to support their conclusions, and to highlight any range of literature or alternative views and equally to advise if and why there is an absence of literature in relation to the cancer type in question, as well as advising upon the need for additional specialist expert reports (such as histopathology).

Once the reports are available, there is then little substitute for holding an early conference with one's team of experts to consider the issues in the round and to ensure that all areas of the claim stack up together. In cancer claims, especially where the claimant's prognosis may be poor or uncertain and in contrast with many other types of claim, a large proportion of the work is necessarily front loaded (and in respect of which the costs budgeting and assessment process is no doubt the subject for a book all of its own!) It is also not uncommon in complex cases, for the expert team, upon meeting and discussing their reports, to amend their views, sometimes in minor form and occasionally more substantially. It is imperative that such changes and the reasons behind them are weeded out and examined at the earliest possible stage, pre-issue and before pleading the case.

Summary

- It is imperative that credible experts are used. When selecting experts, use personal experience, colleague recommendations and don't forget to trawl Lawtel or other resources to ascertain which, if any experts have been discredited in the courts, specifically in relation to cases dealing with the type of cancer with which your case is concerned.

- Which breach of duty expert(s) are instructed will depend upon the factual issues, but even for breach of duty, it is important to know that the claimant had cancer which was detectable at the alleged date of negligence. Oncology evidence is usually required early.

- Tailor the order of your instructions according to your assessment of which elements are likely to be most troublesome.
- Ensure that you have the correct team of experts. Use the MDT for the particular cancer type in question as a checklist.
- Ensure proper planning before instructing the expert.
- Compile a bullet point list identifying each of the key factual and legal issues that the claimant would need to establish in order to succeed in their claim.
- Ensure that the expert is provided with a complete set of well differentiated records and other relevant documents, properly paginated and effectively structured.
- Provide a chronology and clear detail of the client's version of events and any obvious discrepancies identified.
- Ask the expert to address a series of general and then more specific questions focused upon your checklist of the issues that need to be determined.
- Have an early conference with your team.

CHAPTER SIX
CAUSATION

This chapter will consider what steps are required to deal specifically with the factual analysis of causation and how the practitioner should go about testing the expert causation evidence. It aims to guide the practitioner through some of the more common pitfalls and traps for the unwary when analysing expert (principally oncology) evidence and how to address them. In turn, achieving early, thorough, robust and well tested expert evidence, will hopefully improve that party's negotiating and litigation position, as well as making the process simpler in the longer term for the client, expert(s) and lawyers alike.

Factual Causation

Causation is critical and often the most complicated aspect of a cancer claim. The starting point is the same as any personal injury case – what would have happened "but for" the negligence. Or to put it another way, what damage flowed from the negligence.

There are often a number of stages to the factual assessment of causation in a cancer claim. One will always need carefully to examine the timeframe from presentation to referral, referral to investigative tests/scans, test(s) to results and ultimate diagnosis and then to consider the following questions, had the Claimant been referred for investigations earlier.

(a) What investigations would on balance have been conducted?

(b) What would those investigations likely have identified (and specifically when considering x-rays or scans) would a primary tumour likely have been visible?

(c) If a tumour had not been visible following investigation, to what extent if at all, would the Claimant have been monitored and rescanned/re-investigated?

(d) If and when the tumour was visible following investigation, how would it have been staged?

(e) How quickly was the primary tumour likely to have been growing?

(f) How big would the primary tumour likely have been at the date at which a diagnosis ought to have been made and would there likely have been nodal involvement and/or metastatic disease?

(g) If nodal involvement or metastatic disease are likely to have occurred already, would that spread have been detectable at the relevant time or was it likely pre-clinical?

(h) If and when the tumour was visible/detectable following investigation, what treatment would have been recommended (surgery, chemotherapy, radiotherapy, and of which type)?

(i) What treatment would the patient have agreed to undergo? (This is of course, a question for the claimant/family and a review of their attitude to treatment, rather than for the expert, but it is imperative to recognise that just because a patient would have been advised to undergo a certain treatment, it does not necessarily follow that they would have agreed to that course).

(j) What are the prospects that such treatment would have been curative or led to a markedly better outcome (considering Gregg v Scott issues for which see the next chapter)?

(k) What would the Claimant's prospects of survival have been (and if the Claimant remains alive, is there a difference in the risk of recurrence and early death)?

If the Claimant has in fact survived in any event and has the same survival prospects and life expectancy, one will need to ascertain the extent of any additional treatment required by reason of any delay, and the extent of any additional pain, suffering and loss of amenity. Of course, pain, suffering and loss of amenity relates to the physical and psychological consequences of the delay. The latter will often be very significant.

The Pitfalls of Expert Causation Evidence

Grading, staging and doubling times have been discussed in previous chapters. The stage of any particular tumour is fundamentally important in legal as well as medical terms, because it determines the treatment likely to be required and can be translated into a percentage cure/remission rate or average survival time required for arguments on causation. It is frequently in relation to identifying the retrospective size of a primary tumour and/or its likely spread at the date(s) of alleged missed diagnosis that challenges to the expert evidence are based and weaknesses are revealed.

It has already been noted that the very fact that each cancer and its development is unique, working on an individual genetic pattern influenced by the patient's own physiology, in combination with environmental and other factors, makes predictions about its rate of growth and expected course but for any delay, incredibly difficult. That difficulty is magnified when one considers that:

(a) There will usually be no earlier scan or means of comparing the actual size and growth rate of the tumour(s) such that the assessment of growth rate is necessarily speculative, and;

(b) Much of the data upon which oncology experts will assess (at least in part) the growth rate of any particular tumour is based upon average figures drawn from a range of different manifestations of one or more cancer types.

Even with more common forms of cancer where there are well recognised and published studies of doubling times, the experts can usually only give a range of sizes for the tumour at an earlier stage.

There may also be criticisms levelled against evidence or data sets which are based upon patients treated in research studies. It may be suggested that such studies are skewed due to the fact that those entered into the trials usually have a better outcome than the average population, arising from the selection of only the fittest patients to enter such trials or the better treatments available in university departments compared with smaller cancer centres. An article by Kosov, Maxim & Riefler, John & Belotserkovskiy, Maxim. (2016) entitled "Patient Selection Bias in Oncology Clinical Trials" in the Journal for Clinical Studies. 8. 26-28, considers the potential difficulties of selection bias in clinical oncology trials in some detail.

The greatest difficulties are usually with less common cancers where there is a lack of data or where the literature may yield only small numbers of reported cases, reducing the accuracy of the outcome statistics, or the studies may be old studies and potentially cover patients treated with old technologies.

Reliance upon Data from Differing Cancer Types or Reliance upon Data at the Expense of Histology and Symptom Presentation

In any event, it is not usually regarded as appropriate to use doubling times or growth rate data for cancers of a different type than that with which one is dealing. There are further difficulties in calculating the size of metastatic deposits when compared with primary tumours. The practitioner should therefore always check how one's experts have reached their conclusion as to the likely size, staging and spread of the cancer in question.

By way of example, in the High Court judgement in ***P (Deceased) v Sedar (2011) EWHC 1266 (QB) reported on Lawtel***, the Claimant sued as the executrix of the estate of P, who died at the age of 38 of carcinomatosis. Liability was admitted upon the basis that P had not received and therefore missed two hospital appointments which were sent to the wrong address, following her presentation to the GP with a breast lump which was increasing in size. She was not then examined for a further 12 months, by which time she had incurable cancer. A core biopsy showed a Grade 2 lobular cancer. A bone scan showed increased uptake in the vertex of the skull and the right humerus and patchy uptake in the lumber spine with further activity in the right sacroiliac region. She was sadly found to have bone metastases from a primary breast cancer. It was not in dispute that if her breast cancer had been diagnosed in 2000 she would have had good survival prospects. She died, however, as a result of the bone metastases from the primary cancer, which had spread. The key question was whether she would have had bone metastases had she attended the hospital appointments during 2000. If so, it was accepted that she would by that stage, have been incurable and the outcome unchanged.

The experts all agreed that a reasonable estimate of doubling time for the primary breast tumour was 80 days. It was accepted that primary breast cancer grows in the form of 1, 2, 4, 8 and end of life occurs after around 40/41 doublings. It was also agreed that in January 2000 there was no lymph node involvement. The defendant's expert sought to merge a number of sets of data in order to use a process of retrospective "back extrapolation" in relation not only to the primary tumour but also the bone metastases. That was criticised by the claimant's expert team and ultimately rejected by the judge, who was impressed by the claimant's histopathology expert. Of interest, it was noted that:

> "*...back extrapolation is an approximation; it has no real accuracy or precision but it has been used as a result of misdiagnosis, and very often you have to work back. He explained that a good measurement of the tumour is required and a good doubling rate of the tumour; he also said only a few tumours, have exponential growths, which is a third necessity.*"

Moreover, the experts and the judge in turn considered that the defendant's expert's conclusions were based to an inappropriate degree upon assumptions for which there was no evidence (and where none could be ascertained). In addition, there was an attempt to rely upon doubling times for other types of tumour. It was concluded that:

> "*Quoting doubling times for breast metastatic tumours growing in other tissues, such as the lung, have no relevance for metastases growing in bone....*"

Similarly, in ***McGlone v Greater Glasgow Health Board (2013) COSH 34***, the claimant /pursuer had a cervical smear test which identified the presence of abnormal features. She was later diagnosed as having invasive adenocarcinoma of the cervix and, on 30 May 2008, underwent a radical hysterectomy operation. The smear test had identified squamous and glandular endocervical cells with atypical nuclear features suspicious of CIN3 and an atypical glandular component. Two biopsies subsequently suggested at least high grade glandular abnormality. Conservative treatment was by then ruled out due to tumour size. The histology obtained identified residual moderate to well differentiated adenocarcinoma of the endocervix that infiltrated the isthmus and lower part of the body of the uterus with close margins. The total tumour volume was estimated as $29cm^3$. The claim was based upon the alleged misreporting of two prior smear tests in December 2005 and March 2006. A partial admission was made in relation to the 2005 test and a full admission of liability in respect of the March 2006 test. However, it was asserted by the defendant that the pursuer already had, by those dates, invasive cancer such that her treatment course and outcome would have been the same.

The claimant's gynaecological oncologist was of the view that the tumour would have been very small and capable of conservative treatment. In reaching that conclusion, he sought to rely upon published data regarding the growth rates of tumours of various types taken from a paper by Gordon Steel entitled "Growth Kinetics of Tumours" published in 1977 and including data from a range of research papers into the volume doubling times of primary and metastatic tumours. The defenders sought in contrast, to rely upon an interpretation of the pursuer's smears, ultrasounds, histology and symptom profile.

Lord Tyre summarised the defender's criticism of the use of the data relied upon by the pursuer's expert as follows:

> "...*None of the metastases in Steel's table of figures was from a primary cervical carcinoma. In any event metastases were likely to behave differently from primary tumours and in particular were likely to be more aggressive, especially in a favourable environment*

such as the lung. Figures published elsewhere in a textbook by Hall (2000) appeared to show a doubling time for primary adenocarcinomas of 166 days, i.e. more than double the figure of 77 days used by Mr Soutter. They also indicated that metastatic adenocarcinomas grow faster than primary tumours. Steel made the point that tumours were unpredictable and his own figures demonstrated that there was a wide range of doubling times. No allowance had been made for the indolent nature of this particular tumour. There were therefore too many scientific weaknesses for Mr Soutter's estimate to be regarded as reliable...."

Ultimately Lord Tyre agreed with those concerns. He went on to find that:

"...As the defenders submitted, the doubling time of 77 days which Mr Soutter has used is for lung metastases of adenocarcinoma of locations throughout the body, with no positive indication that any of them was from a primary tumour in the cervix. Given the variety of mean doubling times disclosed for lung metastases of adenocarcinoma of different locations (ranging from 33 to 94), it does not appear to me that any reliable conclusion can be drawn from these figures regarding the mean doubling time of lung metastases of cervical adenocarcinoma. In the second place, I am not satisfied that use of a geometrical mean gives a result in which any confidence can be placed for the purposes of the issue arising in the present case... Rates of growth vary from one patient to another and may also vary over time with regard to the same patient. In the case of the pursuer, the defenders' expert witnesses, Dr Williams, Dr Farquharson and Mr Naik, were of the opinion that this was a slow-growing, indolent tumour. This view was based upon histological and other investigations carried out at the time of removal of the tumour, when it was described as moderate- to well-differentiated, with no involvement of pelvic lymph nodes or lympho-vascular space invasion...."

If the statistical evidence had related to the mean growth rate of adenocarcinomas originating in the cervix, then it may well have held rather more weight, although the claimant/pursuer's experts would still have had to deal convincingly with the histology, scan results and symptom profile of this particular lady.

It is therefore important that the legal practitioner ensures that the chosen oncology expert deals with:

i. The range of and most recent data on average tumour growth rates for the specific type of cancer in issue;

ii. Any factors peculiar to the biology of the tumour or the patient which might alter the "average" or the applicability of the mean figures in the specific case;

iii. Whether they are aware of concern that may be raised in relation to the data relied upon, and whether the data is based upon trials which exhibit particular selection bias;

iv. How the question of metastatic spread has been approached, and with what basis in data and/or histopathology evidence.

v. If the claimant were to fall at one or other end of the range supported by the literature, rather than in the middle, what difference would that make to the outcome.

Of course, when evidence is given as to the treatment options likely to have been offered, one should equally ensure that the expert has addressed the state of knowledge at the alleged dates at which such treatment would have been offered.

Life Expectancy Data

It is equally notable that when seeking to prove a reduced life expectancy following a delay in diagnosis, the legal practitioner should be wary of over-reliance upon statistical or epidemiological evidence. Again, that is particularly important in the case of rarer cancers or of applying data or evidence regarding one type of cancer to a case involving a different type of cancer. The pitfalls are illustrated by the fatal accident act case of ***Hague & Rich v Dalzell &Fish [2016] EWHC 2753 (QB) LTL.***

That was a case in which a claim was brought by two executors of the deceased's estate, her mother, and her fiancé. The two defendants were GPs whom the deceased (aged just 25 at her death) had consulted in November 2009 and February 2010. The deceased consulted each of the doctors as she was experiencing abdominal pains and vaginal bleeding. Both defendants admitted that they did not adequately explore the nature and the extent of the bleeding, and that had they done so, the deceased would have been referred and diagnosed with cervical cancer. She would likely have undergone surgery within two to four weeks of referral. In fact, the tumour was not diagnosed until June 2010 and surgery took place seven months after it ought to have been in relation to the first defendant's examination in November 2009 and four months later than ought to have occurred based upon the second defendant's consultation in February 2010. Very sadly, the deceased's cancer came back in October 2010 and she died in November 2011.

The sole issue to be decided by the court was whether, if the deceased had undergone surgery in December 2009 or March 2010, she would have been considered cured, and survived. The claimants' experts argued that the prognosis was good with early diagnosis. Those for the defendant did not agree and argued that given the features of this rare type of cancer, it would have recurred in any event and the deceased would not have survived.

The histology ultimately taken at surgery indicated that the tumour was a poorly differentiated squamous cell carcinoma but with spindle-cell morphology. The tumour also demonstrated high mitotic activity (splitting of cells). Those factors suggested that the tumour had acquired proteins characteristic of a sarcoma, known to act in a clinically aggressive manner, and which would have resulted in the tumour being graded as grade 3. There was no evidence of lymph node infiltration nor of metastatic spread and the margins of clearance achieved at surgery appeared clear, although ultimately, some cancerous cells must have been left behind. As such, by October 2010, the deceased had a further poorly differentiated squamous cell carcinoma of the cervix, measuring some 8.5 x 5.2 x 7.1 cms, making it around 164 cubic centimetres in volume.

Mr Justice Lewis found as fact that at the time when diagnosis ought to have been made, the tumour would have been stage 1b1.

The Judge did not accept attempts made by one of the claimant's experts to use doubling times to interpolate the size and characteristics of the tumour at the time when diagnosis ought to have been made. He commented upon the defendant expert evidence as follows:

> *"..it is inadvisable to use tumour doubling times in this particular tumour because there is no reliable data for the volume doubling time of this tumour or any primary cervical carcinoma growing in situ. He would advise that the growth kinetics of tumour after resection are not always applicable to the primary tumour because of the natural history of primary tumours. However, there is little doubt that this was a rapidly growing tumour.[Professor Wells] considers that [Mr Soutter's] approach is fundamentally flawed because it is not based on any data on cervical tumours and takes no account of host (patient) responses to any particular tumour during the course of the disease..."*

It was agreed that the particular cancer affecting the deceased was very aggressive and rare. The court was advised that there were only 17 such cases in the literature. As such, the judge agreed with the defendants' criticism of the claimant's expert's attempt to take data about the size of an evolved tumour and then to extrapolate backwards over an earlier period to seek to determine the size of the tumour at an earlier stage, especially where there was no reliable data pertaining to the particular type of tumour in issue.

Further, Mr Justice Lewis in consequence also rejected the application of studies on survival chances following treatment for other, more common and less aggressive kinds of cervical squamous cell carcinoma. He went further than that and rejected the Claimant's use of statistical evidence to show that the deceased would have been cured with earlier diagnosis and treatment. He observed that:

> "*The figures are intended to show prospectively the likelihood of survival. They are not designed to be applied retrospectively to predict the likelihood of whether any particular individual would have survived if treated by a particular date.*"

He commented further that:

> "*the statistics are intended to show likely survival rates for a cohort of people ... [evidence that shows] that just under 95 out of a hundred such patients would be alive after 5 years does not assist in determining whether or not a particular patient will be one of the 95 patients who survive or one of the 5 who do not.*"

The statistics also appeared to suggest that at the point of the deceased's actual diagnosis the prospects of survival were between 65.8% and 87.4% depending upon which set of data were used. The very fact that the deceased did not survive at that known point in time indicated to the judge that reliance upon the statistics was flawed, and suggested that some other factor, such as the nature of the tumour, was likely to be relevant in explaining why she died. The dicta of Lord Phillips of Worth Matravers in ***Gregg v Scott [2005] A.C. 176*** and Lord Rodger of Earslferry in ***Sienkiewicz v Greif (UK) Ltd. [2011] 2 A.C. 229*** in relation to the limited circumstances in which it may be possible to infer from statistical evidence that a particular factor was causative of a particular event was also noted. On the facts, Mr Justice Lewis was therefore persuaded by the defendant's expert evidence that:

> "*the tumour in the present case was a highly aggressive, rare form of cancer, namely a sarcomatoid squamous cell carcinoma and that such tumours have a poor prognosis and are likely to recur.*"

The judgment underlines the importance of scrutinising the data relied upon and to consider in terms how the claimant's actual presentation and test results fit with any statistics relied upon. Legal practitioners should not fall into the trap of believing that growth rates or survival prospects can be determined by a review of data alone and any expert who takes such a rigid approach should be challenged. The approach required is very much a holistic one. In cancer cases in particular, it is not enough simply to research and instruct a suitable expert and then rely without question upon what they say in their report. Expert evidence, especially as to causation, and including the literature upon which the expert relies, must be thoroughly and carefully dissected and examined at an early conference. Check first that the literature appended to the report actually says what the expert suggests that it does (believe it or not there are cases where it will not), and secondly, ascertain whether the literature realistically supports the position that your client wishes to advance. The likely staging of the cancer and survival prospects at the point of alleged negligence and at defined stages throughout the case, will need to be addressed step by step. These precautions and stages apply equally to claimant and defendant legal teams.

Summary

- There are a number of stages to the factual assessment of causation in a cancer claim, and which must be approached methodically
- It is frequently in relation to identifying the retrospective size of a primary tumour and/or its likely spread at the date(s) of alleged missed diagnosis that challenges to the expert evidence are based.
- The problems are magnified by the fact that each cancer's development is unique, there are generally no prior scans for comparative purposes, and the data will, at best, provide a range of varying degrees.
- Consider criticism of research study data and whether there is any selection bias.
- Difficulties are more prevalent for rare forms of cancer where there is little or no data or the data is old and outdated.

- It is not usually regarded as appropriate to use doubling times or growth rate data for cancers of a different type with which one is dealing.
- The treatment of metastatic growth is different to primary growth.
- Be equally wary of over-reliance upon statistical or epidemiological evidence in seeking to establish life expectancy and survival rates.
- Carefully examine with the experts in an early conference, how and why they have reached their conclusions.
- Scrutinise the data relied upon and consider how the claimant's actual presentation and test results fit with any statistics relied upon.
- Do not forget to read thoroughly and challenge with your expert the literature upon which they rely and the extent to which the claimant's actual presentation and test results fit with the data.

CHAPTER SEVEN
LEGAL CAUSATION

This chapter will look at how causation can be established in law, once the facts have been analysed. Are there different ways of clearing the hurdle of causation, when do they apply and what evidence is required to do so? The legal practitioner dealing with delayed cancer diagnosis claims requires a clear grasp of the law on causation, and its many faces. Consideration of "but for" causation alone is overly simplistic and risks failure where success is achievable. This chapter will not provide a complete breakdown of the legal provisions, and which could realistically form the basis of a book of its own. However, it will aim to equip the legal practitioner with a basic knowledge of the main types of legal causation and an understanding of when they might be applied (after further research!) in the context of a cancer claim.

Causation in a Clinical Negligence Setting

Care is needed with the concept of causation in the clinical negligence arena generally. The legal concept of causation is distinct from its scientific meaning. For example, if one considers an adverse drug reaction in a patient who is allergic to the medication prescribed and has been documented as having such an allergy, a scientist would say that the reaction was caused by a combination of pre-existing susceptibility, itself with multiple possible causes, together with the administration of medication by the doctor. In law, the function of causation is to attribute legal responsibility for damage, which involves asking whether (1) factual and (2) legal causation has been satisfied. Factual causation has been considered in the previous chapter.

The "but for" test of causation in the clinical negligence sphere has been regarded by some as a prerequisite of liability. In asking "would the damage of which the Claimant complains have occurred but for the wrong of the Defendant", the test aims to eliminate irrelevant causes. If the damage would have occurred in any event the Defendant's conduct is not a "but for" cause. (***Barnett v Chelsea & Kensington Hospital***

Management Committee [1969] 1 QB 428). However, that question is not often, in clinical negligence practise generally, and in cancer claims specifically, capable of an easy answer. Much will therefore depend upon the legal practitioner asking the correct questions of the experts, especially in relation to life expectancy and the prospects of survival.

It is also important to note that when lawyers look at the question of causation, the question is one which ultimately reflects the value of the damages award. For example, compensation for a reduction in life expectancy for a number of years is based upon the financial loss attributable to that period. Equally, where the patient has already died, the loss arising from their death must be assessed primarily in financial terms.

Loss of Chance

In ***Gregg v Scott* (2005) 2 AC 176**, the House of Lords considered the problem of a nine month delay in diagnosis of a lymphoma to the left armpit. The negligent delay allowed the cancer to metastasise so that the claimant's prospects of survival (based upon the expectation of life for another 10 years – the assessment of post treatment survival generally being measured at 5 and 10 years respectively) were reduced. In that case the following findings should be noted:

(a) The statistical evidence in the Claimant's initial expert report had to be altered to take account of further published research, and the fact that the Claimant had in fact survived, which suggested that he had a better prognosis than the norm; and

(b) The judge found that of 100 patients such as the Claimant, at the time of the alleged negligence, 55 would achieve remission, 42 would ultimately survive and 35 would not have had to undergo high dose chemotherapy with stem cell treatment. As such whilst prompt treatment would likely have led initially to remission it would not have produced a better long-term outcome.

(c) At the time of the trial the Claimant had a 25% prospect of disease-free survival for 5 years. There had therefore been a 17% diminution (from 42-25%) in the chance of long-term survival.

(d) The trial judge found that the question of how the Claimant's condition would have developed in the period up until the trial was one of past fact and was not hypothetical so as to put it in the category of quantification.

(e) The trial judge found that the Claimant had failed to prove that the outcome for him, viewed as at the date of the trial, would have been any different.

The claim was initially advanced as a conventional claim for having lost, by reason of the delay, what would otherwise have been a complete cure. That was upon the basis of medical evidence at the time. However, before the trial, it was found that Mr Gregg had a rare type of cancer with a less favourable prognosis. As such, the claim was amended to claim upon the basis that the Claimant's chance of survival was reduced. It was Mr Gregg's case that he should be able to claim for the loss of that chance.

By a majority of 3 – 2 the House dismissed the appeal with costs. The claimant's claim therefore failed. The speech of Lord Phillips MR contains the most detailed analysis of the facts. Interestingly, the House of Lords were critical of the way in which the statistics had been used and interpreted, again highlighting the significance of their assessment. The entirety of the judgement deserves careful reading. As to loss of a chance, the reasoning of the law lords differs as between them, but ultimately, they decided that to bring a successful claim, one must first prove an injury and that the law did not allow for the claim of a loss of chance of survival – either the Claimant can show that he/she would have survived on balance, or not.

The following were clearly important factors in that judgement:

(a) The fabric of the common law would require a radical and wholesale change with unpredictable consequences if allowing recovery for a loss of chance were to be allowed. Lord Phillips indicated that developing special tests of causation on a piecemeal basis to remedy "*perceived injustices in particular factual situations*" was a dangerous strategy.

(b) The financial implications to the NHS weighed heavily with Lord Hoffman.

(c) The fact that if such arguments were allowed they would affect almost all clinical negligence cases and be far from the exceptional departures previously sanctioned and envisaged by cases such as ***Fairchild v Glenhaven*** [2003] 1 AC 32;

(d) The increase in areas of forensic dispute where presently there is consensus, such as the need to assess precisely <u>how</u> probable a given outcome was.

(e) The fact that a workable system which produces occasional injustice but is manageable and capable of operation with some certainty is better in principle than a system aiming for perfection but which would likely become trapped in expensive and lengthy complexity.

(f) The difficulty of reconciling loss of chance arguments with existing and longstanding tortious principles in the personal injury field.

(g) A principled distinction, as per Baroness Hale, between compensation for damaged economic chances, and for personal injury and harm to bodily integrity.

As such, Gregg v Scott would appear to have settled the position as to the basis of a claim for loss of survival prospects for a generation. It should nonetheless be borne in mind that what Gregg v Scott does <u>not</u> say is that once an injury has been proved on the balance of probabilities, damages claims cannot be made upon the conventional loss of chance basis. As such, proof of injury must be proved on the balance of probabilities, rather than loss of a chance below 50%, but thereafter, the loss of chance rules apply unfettered.

Lost Years Claims

It would therefore appear that in the first instance, the parties will need to examine whether and to what extent the claimant can establish that he or she would have survived if the delay had been avoided, in circumstances where, on balance, they will not survive after the delay. If the claimant can establish (based upon appropriate evidence and statistical analysis) that the prospects of survival were above 50% in the absence of delay but have been reduced to a level below 50% at the point of actual diagnosis, the claimant should succeed. That success may be subject to further argument as to future risk and ultimate longevity.

However, is it an end to the matter if the claimant's prospects of survival have always been below 50% but have been reduced further as a result of any negligent delay? Not necessarily.

As Lord Philips and Baroness Hale both noted in ***Gregg v Scott*** *(above),* there was another way for the Claimant to have presented his case which would have been simpler and allowed for success. That was to prove that the delay in diagnosis had reduced his life expectancy by a specified period which the statistics supported on the balance of probabilities. Instead, Mr Gregg had simply claimed that he would have survived.

Baroness Hale put that potential claim in the following way:

> *"There is also the distinct possibility that the delay reduced his life expectancy in the following sense. It is possible that had he been treated when he should have been treated, his median life expectancy then would have been x years, whereas given the delay in treatment his median life expectancy from then is x minus y. This argument requires that the assessment of loss of life expectancy be based on median survival rates: ie those to be expected of half the relevant population at the particular time. If half the men with Mr Gregg's*

> *condition would have survived for x years or over with prompt treatment, and half would have survived for less than x years, then x is the median life expectancy of the group. If the same calculation of life expectancy from when he should have been treated is done in the light of the delay in treatment, the median life expectancy may have fallen. There might therefore be a modest claim in respect of the 'lost years'.*

Such a lost year's claim has also been supported by cases such as ***JD v Melanie Mather* (2013) Med LR 291**. Critically however, such claims can be made during life only. A "lost years claim" is not recoverable by the estate of a deceased claimant in respect of deaths on or after 1 January 1983 pursuant to s 4 Administration of Justice Act 1982.

In ***JD v Melanie Mather* (2013) Med LR 291**, the claimant had consulted the defendant in March 2006 regarding a growth in his groin, which itched, bled when scratched, and seemed to be getting bigger. He was wrongly diagnosed as having a seborrheic wart and told not to worry. The claimant returned to the surgery more than seven months later and was examined by a different doctor who considered that the lesion was probably malignant and removed it. The lesion was confirmed to be cancer and to have spread to the lymph nodes. It later spread to the claimant's lungs and by the trial date, the prognosis was poor. Breach of duty was admitted. It was the claimant's case that had he been diagnosed at the consultation in March 2006 he would have had the tumour excised within two weeks, which would have carried a likelihood of cure and survival. His alternative case was that excision and treatment in March 2006 would have given him a longer life expectancy.

Bean J found as fact that the tumour had a Breslow thickness of 3-4 mm as at March 2006. Further, he considered it rare for a tumour which had not spread at all to give rise to palpable lymph nodes within 7-8 months; such that he considered it likely that the tumour had spread with at least microscopic regional lymph node involvement by March 2006. It would therefore have been a stage IIIB tumour and by October 2006 had become stage IIIC.

Upon those facts the claimant's chances of survival were accepted to fall below 50% as at March 2006, such that his primary claimed failed upon the basis of ***Gregg v Scott***. The claim was amended to rely upon the alternative case set out above, at trial. Bean J noted as follows, having asked for the defendant's expert's comments:

> *"He agreed with the argument in principle, while adding (correctly, of course) the rider that he always tells his patients that each of them is an individual, not the median. He said that, just as he would expect the tumour to have thickened between March and October, so he would expect the degree of nodal spread to have increased. The patient's prospects were worsened, not only in the sense of a reduced chance of survival beyond 10 years, but also in the sense of a reduced expectation of life. He drew my attention to the AJCC survival curve table for patients with stage III melanomas. This shows a median survival time from diagnosis and excision of a Stage IIIC melanoma of approximately 4 years, and a median of 7.5 years for a Stage IIIB melanoma…."*

In view of the fact that the claimant had already done better than the median for a stage IIIC cancer, Bean J determined that his life expectancy had been reduced by three years as a consequence of the delay in diagnosis.

Clearly damages were not to the same extent as would have been the case had the claim successfully established that but for the negligence the Claimant would have survived. Nonetheless, the claimant did recover some damages.

By contrast, in ***Loretta Oliver v Williams* (2013) Med LR 344**, the claimant failed to establish a diminution in life expectancy. That case is a useful reminder of the fact that, in order to establish a diminution in life expectancy, evidence applicable to the material case is required.

The claimant had attended an appointment with the defendant after her symptoms of stomach cramps, bloating and diarrhoea had persisted. The defendant GP decided to have a stool sample analysed. Those results came back as normal. The claimant returned to see the defendant GP two weeks later. He decided to make an urgent referral to hospital for further investigations. The referral letter was either not received or was lost by the hospital and consequently the claimant did not receive an appointment. Because she did not know about the referral, she did not chase up the appointment. Her symptoms persisted and worsened. She attended the surgery again six months later and saw a different GP who urgently referred her to hospital. The hospital diagnosed the claimant with ovarian cancer and she underwent surgery. The claimant subsequently relapsed on two occasions and found chemotherapy harder to tolerate on each occasion. By trial, she was not physically well enough to attend court and her evidence was given by deposition.

On the evidence, the judge, Simeon Maskrey QC found that the defendant had failed to inform the claimant that the urgent referral had been made and that she should watch out for the appointment letter, and in turn, that breach led to a delay in carrying out surgery of five-and-a-half months.

It was agreed between the expert Gynaecologists that the delay would have made no difference to either the staging of the disease or the treatment options that would have been offered. In July 2007 the disease was at stage IIIc and it is probable that in February 2007 it was also at stage IIIc. Management of the disease would have been identical. However, the experts agreed that in February the operating surgeon would not have been able to remove all of the macroscopic tumour. The claimant would have been left with less residual volume of abnormal tissue had she been operated upon in February but (a) some would still have been left behind and (b) the dimensions of material left would still have been less than 2cm.

The claimant's gynaecology expert accepted, in the course of the joint report that:

> "*The body of evidence is relatively weak since the design of the studies which may answer this question is poor*"

And that he was not aware of a single study:

> *"That would specifically address the issue of the prognostic benefit of debulking surgery of varying degrees of success as defined by the volume of residual disease at the end of surgery."*

As such, the judge concluded as follows:

> *"I consider that Mr Herod's analysis was accurate in determining that volume of residual disease in general terms was a prognostic indicator. But given that he could not assess the difference in volume of residual material I do not believe that his estimate is anything more than a 'hunch' or a belief that the claimant has lost the chance of such an improvement. Moreover, I do not believe that the claimant's relatively good response to treatment assists in determining the question. Indeed, the fact that her particular cancer may have been relatively slow growing tends to suggest that Mr Hammond is correct when he says that the difference in volume of residual disease as between February and July would have been slight…."*

It follows that, whilst consideration should always be given, in the case of a living delayed cancer diagnosis claimant, to whether a diminution in life expectancy can be established as an alternative claim, claimant lawyers will need to be astute to the need for cogent evidence to support such a claim and defendant lawyers will be keen to seek out ways of picking apart the literature and clinical factors relied upon by claimant experts in such cases. It would however appear more likely that this type of claim (and the potential to satisfy the legal test of causation where the claimant's overall prospects of survival have at all relevant dates fallen below 50%) will be most likely to succeed where the stage of the cancer has changed during the period of delay. Where, as in the ***Oliver v Williams*** case above, the stage of the cancer and its management would have been wholly unchanged, claimants are likely to face an uphill struggle to prove a discrete diminution in life expectancy.

Material Contribution? The Future?

Following the redefinition of the law on material contribution in *Williams v The Bermuda Hospitals Board (2016) 2 WLR 774* and *Sido John v Central Manchester & Manchester Children's University Hospitals NHS Foundation Trust* (2016) 4 WLR 54, it remains to be seen what impact material contribution arguments may have in delayed cancer claims. However, this would seem to be an area ripe for development in the field of delayed cancer claims, and is a means of establishing causation that all claimant lawyers should now be considering in such claims.

The case of Sido John is certainly a distressing one factually. The claimant, a GP, had a right sided hemiparesis as a result of a childhood infection, which led to him having to use his left hand, as well as suffering from some mobility issues. On 23rd December 2007 he lost his footing on the steps to his flat and fell backwards. He was found two hours later by his neighbour, covered in vomit and in bad shape. He was ultimately taken by ambulance to the Manchester Royal Infirmary and admitted at 6.52am. A CT scan was ordered but repeatedly delayed notwithstanding the onset of symptoms such as confusion and disorientation. He was later moved to another ward and by the time the CT scan was done, it was around 6.5 hours after admission.

The scan identified an acute subdural haematoma causing raised intracranial pressure. Mr John was re-admitted to resus and then transferred to a specialist neurosurgical team. There were further and entirely avoidable delays in transferring the claimant to theatre by ambulance, such that he did not reach surgery until 7.30pm, over four hours after the ambulance was called.

The operation was successful but as a common result of raised intracranial pressure the claimant developed a post-operative intracranial infection and suffered serious cognitive, neuropsychological and psychiatric sequelae.

The findings of the court in relation to breach of duty need not be considered for present purposes. However, causation was key. The claimant argued that he had suffered an extended period of raised intracranial pressure, which in turn, materially contributed to the infection and the physical and psychological deficits with which he now had to live. The defendant asserted that the post-operative infection operated consecutively and concurrently such that the claimant could not rely upon the doctrine of material contribution as set out in the case of ***Bailey v The Ministry of Defence*** **(2008) LS Law Medical 481**. In that case Waller LJ had expressed the principle in this way:

> *"In my view one cannot draw a distinction between medical negligence cases and others. I would summarise the position in relation to cumulative cause cases as follows. If the evidence demonstrates on a balance of probabilities that the injury would have occurred as a result of the non-tortious cause or causes in any event, the claimant will have failed to establish that the tortious cause contributed. Hotson's case exemplifies such a situation. If the evidence demonstrates that 'but for' the contribution of the tortious cause the injury would probably not have occurred, the claimant will (obviously) have discharged the burden. In a case where medical science cannot establish the probability that 'but for' an act of negligence the injury would not have happened but can establish that the contribution of the negligent cause was more than negligible, the 'but for' test is modified, and the claimant will succeed."*

On the contrary, the defendant went on to argue that this was a case of multiple possible causes as in ***Wilsher v Essex Area Health Authority*** **(1988) 2 WLR 557** and as a result of which causation could not be established.

The claimant won comprehensively. The judgement of Picken J is impressive for its clarity and relative brevity. The following conclusions can be drawn from the judgement:

(a) The doctrine of material contribution is capable of application to cases which are not concerned only with a single agency. There is no such restriction within the law and as such, it can apply equally to cases of multiple causative agents.

(b) Clinical negligence cases are distinct from industrial disease cases. In the former, proof of material contribution to *injury* is required, and material contribution to *risk* is insufficient.

(c) Apportionment in clinical negligence cases in which material contribution to injury is made out would be wholly inappropriate, and where it was not merely difficult but is impossible to allot particular loss to a particular cause. As such, the claimant recovers in full if material contribution is made out in cases of indivisible injury (such as cancer).

As such, following the ***John*** and ***Williams*** cases (above), in order for a claimant to succeed he/she must show that:

1. The defendant has been negligent in its care towards the claimant;

2. The negligence has materially contributed to the *injury* rather than the risk of injury, and;

3. It is medically impossible to prove the degree of contribution on a "but for" basis, but;

4. The contribution is more than minimal.

So, to what degree might the doctrine of material contribution assist claimants alleging a delay in the diagnosis of their cancer? That has yet to be seen and the author is unaware of any reported cases upon the subject.

The author is unaware of any cases in which material contribution causation has been argued (successfully or otherwise) at trial. In a fascinating article by Tom Goodhead of 9 Gough Square on 5th February 2016 (entitled "Bailey Survives Bermuda – Material Contribution in Clinical Negligence and appearing on 9 Gough Square's chambers website) and in a now seemingly removed article on Nigel Poole QC's highly informative Learned Friend blog, the facts of a case argued by both barristers and settling successfully during the fourth day of the trial in November

2014 sometime before the ***Williams*** or ***Sido John*** judgements, are useful in demonstrating the way in which material contribution may be approached in these types of claims.

That case of ***Maytum v Abertawe Bro Morgannwg University Health board*** **(unreported)** but covered in the press including the BBC news, The Times and the Daily Mail, concerned a claimant who was referred urgently by her GP for suspected breast cancer when she was just 31. She had a discrete breast lump for six weeks. It is understood that a surgeon at the Princess of Wales Hospital downgraded her referral and treated it as routine, upon the basis that she was under 35 and there were no red flags beyond the presence of the lump.

As a result of the delay the claimant's breast cancer was diagnosed and treated five months later than had the referral been urgent. It appears to have been agreed that upon earlier diagnosis the treatment given would have been exactly the same. The question was however whether, for the claimant, having later relapsed and developed overt metastases, earlier treatment would have been more effective.

The case is interesting for a number of reasons. According to Nigel Poole QC's blog, the use of prognostic tools was expressly dealt with during the case and the experts agreed that the most useful model for assessing likely prognosis in the case was the PREDICT model which the NHS makes available online. The model indicated that in September 2010 when the claimant ought to have had treatment, over 90% of women her age and with her cancer characteristics would have survived for at least 10 years. The corresponding figure from when treatment was actually undertaken was around 82% (as reported by The Times online). Following her relapse, she in fact had a very limited life expectancy.

The defendant's case based upon the expert evidence of Professor Nigel Bundred was that the relapse showed that the claimant's cancer was particularly aggressive, unresponsive to treatment and that she would have relapsed at the same time and with the same ultimate prognosis in any event. The claimant's case as the author understands it, was that PREDICT remained valid and that relapse following actual treatment did not establish likely relapse after earlier treatment. During the delay period, the tumour had grown and the number of axillary nodes involved had increased, both of which were known to be adverse prognostic indicators. The mortality rate had just more than doubled during the period of delay. Further, it was asserted that the delay in diagnosis and treatment had materially contributed to the distinct injury of relapse and the development of overt metastases. The argument was put that even if the cancer had been particularly aggressive, the delay had made a more than minimal contribution to the relapse. The development of overt metastases was an indivisible injury with cumulative causes, including negligent delay.

Plainly, that issue is common to many delay in cancer diagnosis claims and it remains to be seen how that approach is viewed by the courts in practise. It seems unlikely that material contribution could be used effectively to override ***Gregg v Scott*** (see above). However, there would certainly appear to be scope for use certainly in cases where a recurrence has occurred.

It is plain that cancer claims are complex but equally plain that there would appear to be no one test of causation applicable to all such cases. What may apply where prognosis remains favourable after actual treatment may not suit a case where there is a poor prognosis and as such, the practitioner should consider the facts of any one case against all of the potential routes to legal recovery.

Summary

- Causation in delayed cancer claims is complex. Remember that the legal concept of causation is distinct from its scientific meaning.
- Much will therefore depend upon the legal practitioner asking the correct questions of the experts, especially in relation to life expectancy and the prospects of survival.

- Loss of chance – see ***Gregg v Scott* (2005) 2 AC 176** – there is no claim for the loss of chance of survival where the claimant cannot prove that, but for the delay, they would have survived.
- However, if the injury is proved on conventional tests of causation, damages can still be assessed where appropriate, upon a loss of chance basis.
- Lost years – reduction in life expectancy by a defined period. However, beware ***Loretta Oliver v Williams* (2013) Med LR 344.** Evidence rather than an unsupported hunch is required.
- Material contribution – must be to injury rather than to risk of injury in the clinical negligence arena.
- Consider to what extent the doctrine may assist especially where a patient has already suffered a recurrence of their cancer.

CHAPTER EIGHT
CLIENT CARE AND FRAMING THE CASE

This chapter will briefly consider the particularly sensitive nature of delayed cancer diagnosis claims and how the claimant lawyer should manage those complications. It will then go on to look at the way in which delayed cancer claims should be framed and the complexities of litigating a claim for a dying claimant. Those considerations require early assessment, careful discussion and regular review depending upon the claimant's progress.

Sensitivity

It cannot be overstated how important it is to approach any case, but particularly a cancer claim, with due sensitivity. It is easy as lawyers sometimes to forget that we are dealing with human beings, rather than just a disease or points of academic, medical and legal interest.

Many such cases will involve either:

(a) A claimant who currently has cancer and is undergoing treatment for it;

(b) A claimant who is currently in remission from cancer having undergone surgery and/or chemo/radiotherapy and with the threat of recurrence, or;

(c) The family of the person at the heart of the claim, and who has since died as a consequence of their cancer or treatment associated with it.

Every one of those scenarios is fraught with difficulty. In the case of a patient who has died, it can be extremely painful for their nearest and dearest to learn that their loved one would likely have survived and possibly been spared considerable pain and distress in the absence of negligence. It is also difficult for the claimant lawyer to give negative advice where the family may still be grieving and want someone to blame – especially if there has been some breach of duty but an absence of causation. The distinction between those concepts can be hard to take on board.

Moreover, even where the claim has legal merit, explaining the often relatively low level of damages that are likely to be awarded following death requires true sensitivity. As a consequence, to a much greater degree than in other clinical negligence claims, the claimant lawyer will need to manage expectations effectively and advise clients about the potential range of valuations at an earlier stage.

Although for many such claimants, these cases really are not about the money, a large proportion of claimants and/or their families may not want to spend long periods of time and energy (often during already difficult times) dealing with liability and causation only to find out some way down the line that the case may be worth relatively little.

It is therefore imperative that the legal team take time to explain the relevant advice gently, with kindness and in straightforward terms which are not hedged about with medical or legal jargon, but also with professionalism and confidence so as to reassure the client(s) that you know what you are talking about. Clients should, as in all cases, be allowed at the earliest stage to tell their story in their own words, and the issues that are important to them, whether or not they prove to be relevant legally, should be taken on board.

Claimant lawyers in such claims should take clear instructions at the earliest possible stage as to who the legal team are authorised to speak to. Issues of capacity and the potential need for a litigation friend will need to be kept under careful and regular review in cases where the claimant is currently unwell and/or undergoing treatment.

Equally, where the person with cancer is still alive, it is an inevitable part of the construction of the claim that life expectancy evidence will be required. Being confronted in such stark terms with one's own mortality can be both shocking and potentially detrimental to ongoing treatment. The lawyer should therefore ascertain at each stage of the proceedings, precisely what the claimant (where they are the one still suffering with or having suffered with cancer) wishes to know about the detail of the expert evidence. Sometimes, depending upon the claimant (and their families' wishes) such evidence can be given in an addendum to the main report.

Given the sensitivities of such claims, it is also imperative that consideration is given at the earliest possible stage to practical issues including:

(a) Commencing the claim early and if necessary applying for fast track directions, so as to enable requests for interim payments to be made, which might enable the injured party to be made as comfortable as possible (and comforted) during their remaining lifetime;

(b) Considering the way in which the claim needs to be framed, where there is a likelihood (or significant risk) that the living claimant may die during the litigation process.

These discussions and decisions will often need to take place at a much earlier stage than in many other catastrophic injury cases.

Framing the Case – How and When to Bring Proceedings

Ordinarily, if your claimant is alive, the claim is brought in the conventional way as a living personal injury claim, whereas if the claimant has already died, a claim brought by their estate would be commenced under the Fatal Accident Act 1976 as a dependency claim. However, what of the claim where the claimant is alive but with a poor prognosis?

Litigating claims where the claimant is terminally ill, be that due to cancer or to some other illness or disease is fraught with difficulty, not least because of the inevitable uncertainties over the claimant's life expectancy and the course of the disease. It ought not to be forgotten that the life expectancy of the claimant may well change throughout the life of the claim, and should therefore be kept under very careful and regular review with one's experts so that adjustments in both the pursuit and valuation of the claim can be made as soon as practicable.

In the case of ***Thompson v Arnold*** **(2008) PIQR P8**, the defendant doctor had diagnosed a lump in the deceased's breast as benign when in fact it was malignant. The now deceased lady subsequently issued proceedings. However, her schedule did not claim for the lost years. She obtained judgement in default and the claim was later settled, notwithstanding the judge's suggestion at a directions hearing that the claim could be dealt with by way of interim payment with the remaining losses being settled upon death. After the deceased's death, the claimants (widower and children of the deceased) sought to pursue a dependency claim. Langstaff J confirmed that no claim could be brought under the Fatal Accidents Act 1976 by dependants of a victim of a personal injury who later died from their injuries where damages had already been awarded or agreed during the victim's lifetime. As such, if a claim is brought and concluded during the claimant's lifetime, unless in a rare case, the defendant is persuadable otherwise (there is anecdotal evidence of such leniency having occurred), the dependents/estate will ordinarily be deprived of the bereavement award and financial/services claims continuing post mortem (as discussed at Paragraph 20 of Langstaff J's judgement in the above case).

There will undoubtedly be those who, notwithstanding the potential for under compensation where the claim is brought and concluded prior to the claimant's ultimate death, will wish to see as swift and conclusive conclusion to the litigation as possible. Such an approach allows for loose ends to be tied up, for the terminally ill claimant to experience the relief of achieving satisfaction prior to death, and the certainty of some form of security of their dependents thereafter.

That can only be a choice for the claimant themselves but, such a decision should only be made after a considered and sensitive discussion with a claimant who is then aware of all of their options and the pros and cons of each one. As such, the claimant lawyer will need to consider and assess (as far as possible) the financial value of the lost years income claim against the value of any lost dependency claim at an early stage.

The Primary Options

There are a number of options that the claimant lawyer may advise in the case of a terminally ill or dying client, depending upon the client's preferences. As noted previously, as long as the client is aware of the potential for under-compensation and the likely value of the gap in recovery, the only way to achieve true finality is to bring and conclude the claim during the claimant's lifetime.

The most obvious alternative option would be to wait until the claimant dies and then bring a Fatal Accidents Act claim for the dependants. That is probably only likely to be attractive where the claimant's life expectancy is really very short indeed. The disadvantage of that approach is that the claimant themselves will never see a resolution to their claim, and nor will they have the benefit of any damages award or settlement reached as a consequence.

However, those are not the only two potential routes open to the claimant and their legal team. The claim can be brought during the claimant's lifetime, after which an interim payment may be sought before staying the claim and later converting to an FAA claim for the benefit of the dependents (giving credit for the interim payment made during life). As Langstaff J noted in the ***Thompson v Arnold*** case (above) at paragraph 28:

> "*One well recognised route is to seek an interim payment which, in a case in which liability has been admitted, may be equal or nearly equal to the amount of a lifetime award. The fact that it may be, or nearly be, the full amount of such an award does not prevent it being a reasonable proportion of the damages to be expected in the eventual claim (which will by amendment add a claim under the 1976 Act), since in the usual case it follows from what I have set out above that a dependency claim will usually be larger. Authority supports such an approach: Stephenson LJ. recognised in Murray v Shuter [1972] 1 Ll Rep 6, CA that: "delay usually defeats justice; but there are cases, of which claims for head injuries are notoriously an instance, where expedition may work injustice..." when ordering an adjournment of trial, which was otherwise ready and due to be heard, so that the*

dependants of an injured plaintiff whose death was imminent could benefit from the more generous financial compensation likely to be awarded under the Fatal Accidents Act. This principle of adjournment in appropriate cases, in order to secure the benefits of this Act, may be combined with an interim payment."

Similarly, the claim may be brought during the claimant's lifetime, with resolution of some heads of loss such as PSLA and past losses, whilst staying assessment of claims such as future earnings and care until after death. After death, the claim would then be restored and converted to an FAA claim for dependency.

The likelihood is that those options will only be appropriate where there is already a full admission of liability.

Provisional Damages

One other option is to consider a claim for provisional damages. Section 32A Senior Courts Act 1981 provides as follows:

"This section applies to an action for damages for personal injuries in which there is proved or admitted to be a chance that at some definite or indefinite time in the future the injured person will, as a result of the act or omission which gave rise to the cause of action, develop some serious disease or suffer some serious deterioration in his physical or mental condition.

(2) Subject to subsection (4) below, as regards any action for damages to which this section applies in which a judgment is given in the High Court, provision may be made by rules of court for enabling the court, in such circumstances as may be prescribed, to award the injured person—

(a) damages assessed on the assumption that the injured person will not develop the disease or suffer the deterioration in his condition; and

(b) further damages at a future date if he develops the disease or suffers the deterioration…."

The manner in which claims for provisional damages are to be made and adjudicated upon are further considered within CPR Part 41 and its attendant practice direction (PD 41A). As such, a provisional damages award does not preclude a future FAA claim. On the contrary, its purpose is to preserve a future claim. If the claimant has a poor life expectancy supported by expert evidence and literature, there would plainly be a chance (and which has been interpreted as needing only to be more than fanciful) of serious deterioration at an indefinite time in the future. As such, that approach would allow resolution of the claim during the claimant's lifetime upon the assumption that he/she survives, with a resurrection of the claim and assessment of damages for dependency after death.

There must generally be a clear-cut event which 'triggers' the application for further damages as per ***Wilson v MOD*** **[1991] 1 All E R 638 (644h)** in which Scott Baker LJ stated that the section envisages a clear and severable risk rather than a continuing deterioration. The latter scenario has tended to be argued in personal injury claims in the presence of degenerative osteoarthritis arising from an injury. However, is the risk of deterioration in a cancer sufferer who already has a terminal diagnosis "continuing deterioration" or a "clear and severable risk"? In the usual way, defendants will no doubt seek to challenge provisional damages claims which are due to deteriorations capable of sensible prediction at the point of litigation.

Nonetheless, it is certainly true that in cases where the claimant is not terminally ill but there is a risk of recurrent disease and/or additional risks arising from treatment, the courts have been willing to make orders for provisional damages. They are frequently utilized in disease litigation where claimants with asbestos related disease have a risk of developing lung cancer and/or mesothelioma. Further, in ***Thurman v Wiltshire and Bath Health Authority (1997) BMLR 63***, the claimant, having suffered from cervical cancer, the diagnosis of which had been delayed, required termination of her then twelve week pregnancy, hysterectomy and radiotherapy followed by an implant of caesium into her vagina. She made a good physical recovery. However, the court ordered provisional damages upon the basis of three future risks, namely the risk of recurrences of cancer further to her cervical carcinoma, osteoporosis consequent upon radiotherapy and interference with urinary function as a result of radiotherapy. Provisional damages in respect of the first risk (of recurrent cancer) was lifelong and without limit, whereas the risks arising from radiotherapy were limited to a ten year longstop.

By contrast, in the recent case of ***XX v Whittington Hospital NHS Trust (2018) PIQR Q2,*** Sir Robert Nelson, sitting in the High Court, was tasked with considering a delayed diagnosis of cervical cancer claim. As a result of the delay the claimant, aged 29, developed an invasive stage IIB cancer requiring surgery and chemo radiotherapy. She suffered a total loss of fertility, but wished to have a family, as a result of which she underwent egg harvesting. She also suffered bowel and bladder injuries, sexual dysfunction, early menopause and anxiety and depression. The case also considered interesting issues such as the extent of recoverability of surrogacy expenses, and evidence in respect of reduced life expectancy. The latter point concerned the defence submission that life expectancy was reduced, presumably in order to reduce the quantum of damages for ongoing losses. The court rejected that argument for lack of any proper evidence. However, for present purposes the interesting issue is the consideration given to an award of provisional damages. It was agreed that provisional damages should be ordered for the risk of radiation enteritis, but the claimant also sought provisional damages in respect of a risk of deterioration in her mental condition should surrogacy completely fail. The risk of a catastrophic response to such events was put at around 30-40%, but the claimant's expert considered that one year's worth of treatment would likely be successful. The judge declined to award provisional damages to account for that risk, noting that:

> "*I am clear that the risk of deterioration at 30 – 40% even though it only arises if the surrogacy fails, is real rather than fanciful. The second limb of the test presents a more difficult problem. It is difficult, in my judgement, to hold that a deterioration which may be*

> *severe but which is likely to be temporary and treated successfully in about one year can properly be regarded as serious under the test for provisional damages. This is not one of those rare cases where the normal rules for the awarding of damages should be displaced. The Claimant can be properly compensated within the normal rules. There is also the problem, which may arise, of establishing the origins of a particular psychological condition or its exacerbation…."*

It should also be noted that the High Court have considered the issue of whether a deterioration in the claimant's condition likely to result in a decrease rather than an increase in the global damages award should act as a bar to an award of provisional damages. In real terms, if provisional damages were to be awarded in such a case, the claimant would recover a higher award, probably most significantly in respect of lost earnings, upon the assumption that deterioration would not occur, and then be able to return for further damages in the future if the deterioration occurred, notwithstanding the fact that early demise effectively invalidated the basis of the award first made. This lacuna is not provided for within section 32A.

The issue was considered in the case of ***Molinari v Ministry of Defence (1994) PIQR Q33*** by Mr W Crowther QC sitting as a deputy High Court judge. The claimant was an employee at the royal naval dockyards. He was exposed to ionising radiation as a result of which he developed leukemia. He underwent intensive treatment and was unlikely to return to his job. The prognosis was not optimistic with a 12-20% chance of relapse which would lead to extensive treatment and inevitable death.

The judge used an extreme example to illustrate the unusual position set out above. He concluded that in Mr Molinari's particular case:

> "*Putting the matter at its lowest, I have no doubt that any injustice that the defendants may suffer from an award of provisional damages is far outweighed by the potential injustice to the plaintiff in not making such an award and accordingly, I propose to award provisional damages….*"

However, he left open the possibility that, in an extreme case it might be proper for a court to refuse to award provisional damages where the potential injustice to the paying party would outweigh the injustice to the claimant of any final award. As such, the question has not been answered definitively.

The Law Commission in their September 1994 consultation paper in respect of "Structured Settlements and Interim and Provisional Damages, No 224, considered whether there was a need for reform in that regard and having made reference to the Molinari case. They decided that no such reform was needed, and that:

> "*The provisional damages regime was developed as a palliative to reopening and reviewing cases...In any event, we consider that the regime allows a valuable flexibility of approach, which the judge in this case used entirely appropriately. Where clear injustice to a defendant would result from a provisional award, and the plaintiff would suffer less injustice from a traditionally assessed lump sum, the traditional approach should be taken....*"

The author is unaware of any reported cases in which the issue has since been determined and decided in the defendant's favour. As such, it remains open for defendants to argue that provisional damages are inappropriate even where there is an agreed risk of deterioration, where the same would result in a significant reduction in the global damages award payable. The level at which the balance of justice tips in favour of the defendant is unclear.

There is however, one further way in which the terminally ill claimant may choose to bring their claim, but which has yet, to the author's knowledge, to be tested in reported practise.

Periodical Payments?

In theory at least, there would appear to be no reason why settlement of a dying claimant's claim could not be resolved during life, to include a future dependency claim, by a periodical payments order.

This option has been much debated in articles by Christopher Melton QC (J.P.I. Law 2008, 4, 285-290) and by Nigel Poole QC in the course of his Learned Friend blog on 2nd October 2012, both of which ought to be read in full. There is further some indication in the ***Thompson v Arnold*** case noted above, that PPOs might, in a case brought after their introduction, be determined upon that basis.

By virtue of section 2 (1) Damages Act 1996 and coming into force on 1st April 2005, in every case which includes an award of future pecuniary loss as a result of personal injury, the court has a mandatory duty to consider whether to make an order for periodical payments. That would apply to most cancer claims.

The power to make a PPO which bridges death is plain from a review of the CPR. Part 41.8 (1) and (2) state respectively that any such order must specify that the annual future pecuniary losses are to be paid *"for the duration of the claimant's life, or such other period as the court orders...."* and that:

> *"Where the court orders that any part of the award shall continue after the claimant's death, for the benefit of the claimant's dependants, the order must also specify the relevant amount and duration of the payments and how each payment is to be made during the year and at what intervals."*

Of course, CPR 41.8(3) also allows for payments to be stepped. The Practice Direction to CPR Part 41 and the Department for Constitutional Affairs (DCA) Guidance on Periodical Payments issued in 2005 provides some insight into how such an order might work. In theory at least, such an order ought to allow for:

(a) Recovery of damages including a dependency claim prior to the claimant's death;

(b) Potential recovery of services claims during the lost years (which are otherwise not permitted) and lost years earnings claims without the increased reduction for expenses currently provided for in ***Phipps v Brooks Dry Cleaning Services Ltd*** **(1996) PIQR Q100**;

(c) (c) A more accurate apportionment of financial losses, which are adaptable to changing situations.

However, there are potential pitfalls and obvious complexities.

Taxation

The most complicated issue is likely to be in relation to taxation. PPOs during the claimant's lifetime are tax exempt. As Christopher Melton QC points out in his article "*Periodical Payments and Terminal Disease*" as referenced above, the DCA guidance and a strict interpretation of the Income Tax (Trading and Other Income) Act 2005 and its predecessor, the Income and Corporation Taxes Act 1988, suggest that tax exemption will not survive the claimant. In the case of the DCA guidance, it is explicit in stating that:

> "*The tax exemption applies only to the person entitled to the damages under the agreement or order (i.e. the claimant). If the periodical payments carry on after the death of the claimant for the benefit of the claimant's dependants, they will lose their tax free status and will be liable for income tax....*"

The issue appears to be who "*the person entitled to the damages under the agreement*" is, and it will be noted that Mr Melton QC describes having received rather more positive advice from the HMRC, depending upon the terms of the order and for whose benefit the payment is expressed to be made. It may therefore be a sensible first step in any such case for the claimant's legal team to make enquiries of HMRC (preferably supported in writing) if a PPO is considered to be potentially advantageous, although reliance upon telephone advice without any formal undertaking is unlikely to prove attractive.

Plainly, without tax exemption for dependency damages, any such order is likely to be significantly less attractive. It is perhaps inevitable that financial advice will need to be sought in all such cases, both in relation to the tax implications of a PPO, but also in relation to the broader financial consequences of the alternative options available.

Drafting Complexities

There would appear to be no obvious bar (at least within the legislative provisions and the CPR) to any such order in cases where liability is not admitted or agreed on an undiscounted basis, although in that scenario, one would envisage greater difficulty in determining the level and time-frame of stepped payments such as accurately to reflect the liability position.

Drafting a PPO for a terminally ill claimant is likely to be fraught with difficulty even where liability is not in issue, and in any case, there may well be situations where the imponderables affecting the assessment of future dependency will be so extensive that a PPO will be inappropriate. Defendants may well be averse to PPOs in these cases, and may use arguments about the complexities of assessment and drafting and the potential for an unwieldy order, to challenge any claimed intention to apply for a PPO in a delayed cancer claim.

One such problem may come in determining the date of the claimant's death such as to trigger the stepped change in payments (and which requires a date to be specified pursuant to CPR 41.8(3). Would it be sufficient simply to specify that the change should apply upon the claimant's death? That has yet to be seen. Further stepped changes would then, presumably, be required when the dependency of each dependent comes to an end, and would likely need to be apportioned for the benefit of each such dependent within the wording of the order.

There are equally likely to be substantial difficulties (although arguably not insurmountable in some cases) in determining the level of dependency in circumstances where the date of the claimant's death is uncertain. To do so would require the making of predictions, and which are likely to become less and less accurate the further into the future one seeks to gaze.

Further, as Nigel Poole QC opines, there would have to be some mechanism by which the defendant's position is protected should the claimant later die from another, unrelated cause (disease or accident).

Plainly, which option is suitable in any one case will depend upon a range of factors including whether liability is in dispute, the extent to which the claimant's life expectancy is now limited, whether there are or are likely to be dependants, the confidence in the prognosis, the likely value of any lost years claim as against a potential FAA claim, how amenable the defendant is, the client's wishes and anxieties, the defendant's preferences and any issues with proof of the attribution of future death to the negligent delay. The list is extensive.

Further, one must also bear in mind that if settlement is reached including recovery for a protected party in relation to an FAA claim which could not be brought at present because the Claimant is still alive, court approval will still be needed.

There is no one size fits all approach to these claims, and the claimant's legal team in particular, will need to give careful thought to the benefits and disadvantages of these framing options from the outset. Defendants will need to keep an eye to the way in which the claim against them is pleaded and marshal their evidence in response as soon as is practicable.

Summary

- Cancer claims are particularly sensitive and require careful and considerate management.
- The claimant lawyer will need to manage expectations effectively and advise clients about the potential range of valuations at an earlier stage.
- Take clear instructions at the earliest possible stage as to who the legal team are authorised to speak to and precisely what the living cancer claimant wants to know about their life expectancy and which details they do not wish to be privy to.

- Keep capacity issues under regular review where appropriate.
- Litigating claims where the claimant is terminally ill, is fraught with difficulty, not least because of the inevitable uncertainties over the claimant's life expectancy and the course of the disease.
- Consider at the earliest possible stage how the claim might best be framed for the protection of the terminally ill claimant and their dependents.
- Ensure that the claimant is given the appropriate information about the benefits and disadvantages of each option and the financial implications so as to allow them to make an informed decision.
- Bringing a living PI claim and settling it during the claimant's lifetime may not always be appropriate. In most cases the claimant will have to forego the bereavement award and future financial and services dependency claims.
- A claim may be brought after the claimant's death as an FAA claim but the terminal claimant will not personally see a resolution of the claim or gain any benefit from the damages awarded.
- There are options in some cases for bringing the claim during the claimant's lifetime and staying it after receipt of an interim payment or settlement of some heads of (past) loss until after death;
- Consider provisional damages, whether the claimant is dying or if there is a risk of recurrence.
- Periodical payment orders are a possible means of resolution. The rules would appear to allow such recovery but they are fraught with difficulties, principally in relation to taxation and the drafting of imponderables, and are untested in this field.

MORE BOOKS BY LAW BRIEF PUBLISHING

A selection of our other titles available now:-

'A Practical Guide to Immigration Law and Tier 1 Entrepreneur Applications' by Sarah Pinder
'A Practical Guide to Unlawful Eviction and Harassment' by Stephanie Lovegrove
'In My Backyard! A Practical Guide to Neighbourhood Plans' by Dr Sue Chadwick
'A Practical Guide to the Law Relating to Food' by Ian Thomas
'A Practical Guide to the Ending of Assured Shorthold Tenancies' by Elizabeth Dwomoh
'Commercial Mediation – A Practical Guide' by Nick Carr
'A Practical Guide to Financial Services Claims' by Chris Hegarty
'The Law of Houses in Multiple Occupation: A Practical Guide to HMO Proceedings' by Julian Hunt
'A Practical Guide to Unlawful Eviction and Harassment' by Stephanie Lovegrove
'A Practical Guide to Solicitor and Client Costs' by Robin Dunne
'Artificial Intelligence – The Practical Legal Issues' by John Buyers
'A Practical Guide to Wrongful Conception, Wrongful Birth and Wrongful Life Claims' by Rebecca Greenstreet
'Occupiers, Highways and Defective Premises Claims: A Practical Guide Post-Jackson – 2nd Edition' by Andrew Mckie
'A Practical Guide to Financial Ombudsman Service Claims' by Adam Temple & Robert Scrivenor
'A Practical Guide to the Law of Enfranchisement and Lease Extension' by Paul Sams
'A Practical Guide to Marketing for Lawyers – 2nd Edition' by Catherine Bailey & Jennet Ingram
'A Practical Guide to Advising Schools on Employment Law' by Jonathan Holden

'Certificates of Lawful Use and Development: A Guide to Making and Determining Applications' by Bob Mc Geady & Meyric Lewis
'A Practical Guide to the Law of Dilapidations' by Mark Shelton
'A Practical Guide to the 2018 Jackson Personal Injury and Costs Reforms' by Andrew Mckie
'A Guide to Consent in Clinical Negligence Post-Montgomery' by Lauren Sutherland QC
'A Practical Guide to Running Housing Disrepair and Cavity Wall Claims: 2nd Edition' by Andrew Mckie & Ian Skeate
'A Practical Guide to the General Data Protection Regulation (GDPR)' by Keith Markham
'A Practical Guide to Digital and Social Media Law for Lawyers' by Sherree Westell
'A Practical Guide to Holiday Sickness Claims – 2nd Edition' by Andrew Mckie & Ian Skeate
'A Practical Guide to Inheritance Act Claims by Adult Children Post-Ilott v Blue Cross' by Sheila Hamilton Macdonald
'A Practical Guide to Elderly Law' by Justin Patten
'Arguments and Tactics for Personal Injury and Clinical Negligence Claims' by Dorian Williams
'A Practical Guide to QOCS and Fundamental Dishonesty' by James Bentley
'A Practical Guide to Drone Law' by Rufus Ballaster, Andrew Firman, Eleanor Clot
'Practical Mediation: A Guide for Mediators, Advocates, Advisers, Lawyers, and Students in Civil, Commercial, Business, Property, Workplace, and Employment Cases' by Jonathan Dingle with John Sephton
'Practical Horse Law: A Guide for Owners and Riders' by Brenda Gilligan
'A Comparative Guide to Standard Form Construction and Engineering Contracts' by Jon Close
'A Practical Guide to Compliance for Personal Injury Firms Working With Claims Management Companies' by Paul Bennett
'A Practical Guide to the Landlord and Tenant Act 1954: Commercial Tenancies' by Richard Hayes & David Sawtell
'A Practical Guide to Personal Injury Claims Involving Animals' by Jonathan Hand

'A Practical Guide to Psychiatric Claims in Personal Injury' by Liam Ryan

'Introduction to the Law of Community Care in England and Wales' by Alan Robinson

'A Practical Guide to Dog Law for Owners and Others' by Andrea Pitt

'Ellis and Kevan on Credit Hire – 5th Edition' by Aidan Ellis & Tim Kevan

'RTA Allegations of Fraud in a Post-Jackson Era: The Handbook – 2nd Edition' by Andrew Mckie

'RTA Personal Injury Claims: A Practical Guide Post-Jackson' by Andrew Mckie

'On Experts: CPR35 for Lawyers and Experts' by David Boyle

'An Introduction to Personal Injury Law' by David Boyle

'A Practical Guide to Claims Arising From Accidents Abroad and Travel Claims' by Andrew Mckie & Ian Skeate

'A Practical Guide to Cosmetic Surgery Claims' by Dr Victoria Handley

'A Practical Guide to Chronic Pain Claims' by Pankaj Madan

'A Practical Guide to Claims Arising from Fatal Accidents' by James Patience

'A Practical Approach to Clinical Negligence Post-Jackson' by Geoffrey Simpson-Scott

'A Practical Guide to Personal Injury Trusts' by Alan Robinson

'Employers' Liability Claims: A Practical Guide Post-Jackson' by Andrew Mckie

'A Practical Guide to Subtle Brain Injury Claims' by Pankaj Madan

'The Law of Driverless Cars: An Introduction' by Alex Glassbrook

'A Practical Guide to Costs in Personal Injury Cases' by Matthew Hoe

'A Practical Guide to Alternative Dispute Resolution in Personal Injury Claims – Getting the Most Out of ADR Post-Jackson' by Peter Causton, Nichola Evans, James Arrowsmith

'A Practical Guide to Personal Injuries in Sport' by Adam Walker & Patricia Leonard

'The No Nonsense Solicitors' Practice: A Guide To Running Your Firm' by Bettina Brueggemann

'Baby Steps: A Guide to Maternity Leave and Maternity Pay' by Leah Waller

'The Queen's Counsel Lawyer's Omnibus: 20 Years of Cartoons from The Times 1993-2013' by Alex Steuart Williams

www.ingramcontent.com/pod-product-compliance
Lightning Source LLC
LaVergne TN
LVHW022107200926
848481LV00003B/1082
9781911035985